Swapna Liddle's love for the city of Delhi, and in particular Shahjahanabad, led her to write a PhD thesis on its cultural and intellectual life in the nineteenth century. Today she seeks to raise awareness about the city's historic precincts, mainly through her work for the Indian National Trust for Art and Cultural Heritage (INTACH). She is the author of *Delhi: 14 Historic Walks*.

Chandni Chowk
The Mughal City of Old Delhi

SWAPNA LIDDLE

SPEAKING TIGER PUBLISHING PVT. LTD
4381/4, Ansari Road, Daryaganj,
New Delhi—110002, India

First published in India by Speaking Tiger in hardback 2017

Copyright © Swapna Liddle 2017

Illustrations: Courtesy Swapna Liddle's collection

ISBN: 978-93-86338-06-8
eISBN: 978-93-863380-5-1

10 9 8 7 6 5 4 3 2 1

Typeset in Cardo by SÜRYA, New Delhi
Printed at Thomson Press India Ltd.

All rights reserved.
No part of this publication may be reproduced, transmitted, or stored in a retrieval system, in any form or by any means, electronic, mechanical, photocopying, recording or otherwise, without the prior permission of the publisher.

This book is sold subject to the condition that it shall not, by way of trade or otherwise, be lent, resold, hired out, or otherwise circulated, without the publisher's prior consent, in any form of binding or cover other than that in which it is published.

Contents

Acknowledgements vii

Foreword ix

Introduction xiii

Conceiving the City 1

The Imperial Capital 25

Time of Troubles 47

The East India Company's Administration 73

The Revolt and its Aftermath 95

Shahjahanabad in the Twentieth Century 122

Shahjahanabad Today 150

Notes 160

Acknowledgements

My study of the history of Delhi is based on the work of a large number of scholars. In the list are more books and articles than can be included in specific footnotes, and many lectures and conversations from which I have benefited. This work is an acknowledgement of all the scholarly research that has been done on the subject. For my own research specifically, I would like to thank my PhD supervisor Mukul Kesavan, for his support and encouragement, but most of all because he always asked the right questions.

The shape this book has taken is directly owing to Renuka Chatterjee, who commissioned it and commented on the drafts. Maithily Doshi's work on the layout has given it a polished finished form. Gourab Banerji departed from his usual policy of careful distance from my work, to make helpful comments and suggestions. I would like to thank them all.

I also gratefully acknowledge the support of YES BANK and YES Institute, who have contributed to the publication of this book.

Foreword

YES INSTITUTE IS PROUD TO SUPPORT EMINENT HISTORIAN, Swapna Liddle's *Chandni Chowk: The Mughal City of Old Delhi* which brings to life the majestic history of Old Delhi and tracks the trajectories of the old city which have shaped North India's cultural landscape. As someone who has grown up in Delhi, amidst all its fascinating heritage and monuments, I can truly identify with the author's narrative of the multifaceted, vibrant and rich history of the city.

At YES BANK, we are dedicated to the promotion, development and conservation of India's cultural heritage through our YES Culture initiative, which is an integral part of our practicing think-tank, YES Institute. At YES Institute, glocalisation of ideas is driving new age innovations and solutions for India's socio-economic growth and development. We are indeed uniquely positioned to drive socio-economic development through promotion of India's creative and innovative culture forms.

Taking lessons from Delhi's grand intellectual and cultural history can be truly beneficial for the development of our country. YES Institute and YES Culture's initiatives and efforts are focused on India's rich and diverse heritage. Our sustained efforts in this vital area are aimed at promoting national pride and developing India into a truly community-driven, sustainable destination.

Swapna Liddle's lucid style succeeds in addressing all of us in an easy manner and the vast range of sources that she draws on brings the stories of Old Delhi alive. Her love for the city of Delhi shines through and this is echoed in her long-standing work at INTACH. This work has significantly shaped conservation and heritage education; it has also spearheaded heritage awareness in India.

Old Delhi embodies centuries of growth and diverse leadership within its historic tapestry. This has resulted in an environment of new juxtaposed with old, and several different communities living together. The heritage structures and people that live in these landscapes come together to represent the city's rich history, traditions and beautiful craftsmanship.

Promoting citizen engagement with our tangible and intangible heritage must make heritage accessible to all. Civil society participation and awareness of our heritage is vital for the preservation and conservation of these heritage sites.

I am confident this unique book will encourage you to relish and visit Old Delhi's cultural treasures and appreciate them as important assets in the life of our national capital.

New Delhi, November 2016   RANA KAPOOR
Managing Director & CEO, YES BANK
and Chairman, YES Institute

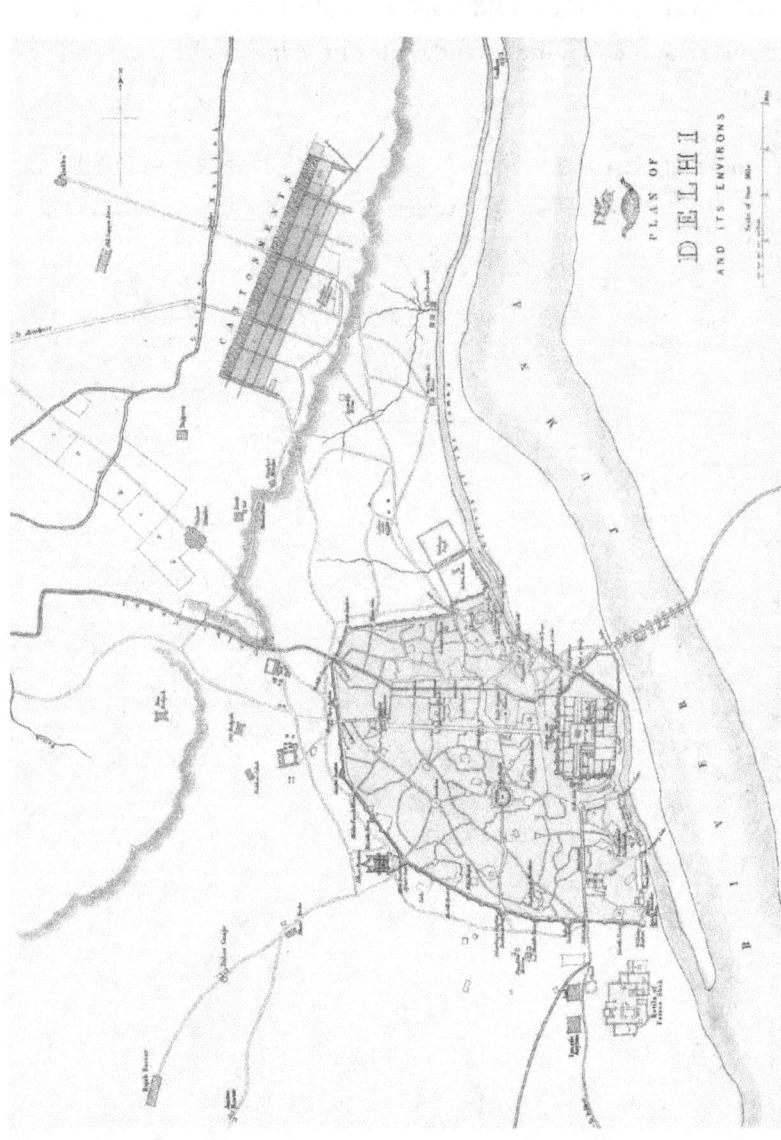

Map of Shahjahanabad and its surroundings, published in 1857.

Introduction

THIS BOOK IS ABOUT ONE OF THE GREAT HISTORIC CITIES OF THE world, and spans some three centuries of its past. Writing the history of a city such as Delhi is both exciting and challenging. Delhi has had a rich urban past, and what is particularly interesting is the fact that at different points of time several different sites were chosen by various political powers to found new settlements or cities. It is commonly said that there have been seven historic cities of Delhi. The truth is, there have actually been more than seven different sites that have been developed as capitals by ruling powers.

Of these, the seventeenth-century Mughal city of Shahjahanabad is of particular interest for two main reasons. Firstly, its street plan and major buildings are still mostly intact, which enables us to understand its layout and design. Secondly, it is still a living city. Though the lives of the people inhabiting it have changed over the centuries, the city's markets, lanes and courtyard houses, to quite an extent, continue to be used as they were in Shahjahan's time.

Today, Shahjahanabad has been subsumed under the gigantic sprawl of metropolitan Delhi. On the map of modern Delhi, it occupies a fairly small dot. Yet it has an identity that is distinct. Popularly known as Chandni Chowk, or Old Delhi, its name conjures up romantic narrow streets, a variety of street food and exotic markets. And increasingly, not only tourists but residents of other parts of Delhi want to experience this city and its culture in all its richness. Proof of this lies in the popularity of the many different historic tours, heritage walks, food walks, photography workshops and the like, that focus on this historic precinct.

While it is interesting to explore the contemporary space that is Chandni Chowk today, it is equally fascinating to explore its history, and in fact the one complements the other. My own engagement with this city has been at multiple levels. Many years of personal exploration in its intricate lanes have led me to a familiarity and appreciation of the physical space of the city, and of its contemporary culture. At another level, a PhD thesis on the intellectual and cultural life of nineteenth century Delhi prompted me to look at this city's past with the rigour of an academic.

My work with the Delhi Chapter of the Indian National Trust for Art and Cultural Heritage (INTACH) has involved a concern with the need to preserve Shahjahanabad's many historic structures. An interesting project with which I was involved, was the production of a detailed dossier that formed part of the application to the United Nations Educational, Scientific and Cultural Organization (UNESCO), for inclusion of Shahjahanabad on the list of World Heritage Cities. The writing of the historical background that was part of this dossier prompted me to examine closely and think deeply about what was special about this historic city. Though that project did not reach fruition, the work on it has been rewarding in other ways, and deserves to be shared.

In a way, this book is the result of my interaction with Shahjahanabad on these various planes. For many years I have been leading heritage walks through Shahjahanabad, with a view to raising awareness about the need to preserve its rich history and traditions. An important part of the narrative on such walks is the history of the city's many sites. Events and characters from different eras of the history of the city are intimately connected to the spaces one walks through today. Invariably, an important question that is posed to a walk leader at the end of the walk is—is there a book where I can read about the history of Shahjahanabad?

It is a question I find hard to answer. There are many books that have been written on Shahjahanabad. On the one hand, there are richly illustrated coffee table books that deal with some aspects of its history, culture and architecture, through pictorial essays. At the other end of the spectrum there are books that examine the city from a planning perspective—its design, layout, use and evolution. Then there are history books that have dealt in detail with the foundation of the city, its major buildings and neighbourhoods. There are some books that deal with major historical events, or with movements and institutions, such as books on the Revolt of 1857, on the freedom movement, on various educational institutions. For the greater part however, the story of the people of the city, their lives, and the major events that took place within the walls of Shahjahanabad can only be gleaned from stray references in history books and articles, which are usually academic works that do not have a general readership.

This book seeks to answer the need to give the general reader a reliable history of the city, its people and major events. The process of planning and writing it involved certain choices and constraints. One of them was the timeframe. I have chosen to talk about the city from the time of its foundation through the next three hundred or so years—uptil Independence and Partition. The next two choices were related—what should be the style of writing and emphasis? I wanted to write in a jargon-free, easy-to-read style that would be accessible to a general readership. This necessarily also meant that explicit articulation of theoretical arguments be largely kept out, and the narrative should unfold as a story, in a chronological scheme.

While I had chosen to write for a general readership, I was equally determined not to compromise on the rigour of scholarship. The writing had to be based on well-researched history. The wide scope of the work means that not all the primary research is mine; much of it is based on the works of others available to me through published writings. My own primary research is reflected particularly in Chapter 4 and a large part of Chapter 5, which draw heavily on

A quaint European interpretation of an important Mughal court ritual—the weighing of the emperor. A print published in England in 1782.

my unpublished thesis. In either case, the sources of my information are clearly set out in reference notes. These give the interested reader an opportunity to follow up my research with further reading, but they are not essential to an enjoyment of the book.

How a book is written, what is included and what left out, are necessarily subjective choices. I have taken the sources that were available to me, and tried to weave an interesting narrative. If certain moments in history occupy a disproportionate amount of space on the pages—such as the Revolt of 1857, it is because they are interesting as well as significant—a major turning point in history. Many other incidents may not have had much impact on the course of events, but are worth detailing because they are illustrative of society at a particular point of time. One example, of many in this book, is how the people of the city reacted to the death of Emperor Farrukh Siyar. In addition, I have tried to make the narrative interesting through the use of a fair number of quotes, which include the comments of European visitors, Mughal court historians, and even poetry, as a reflection of public opinion. I hope that through this device, readers get an insight into the kinds of sources that form the basis of this history.

Finally, I trust this book will appeal to a wide range of aims and interests. For those intrigued by Mughal history or the history of North India generally, a study of its major capital city is definitely of interest. For those interested in exploring Old Delhi as it is now, an understanding of its history will certainly enhance their experience. It will also appeal to all those who simply like a good story.

SWAPNA LIDDLE
New Delhi, September 2016

The broad street in front of the Red Fort, with a channel of water running down the middle. A newspaper illustration from 1857.

Conceiving the City

THROUGH HISTORY THERE HAVE BEEN SEVERAL GRAND EMPIRES, and they have frequently provided the bases on which great civilizations have been built. The Persian, Roman, Ming, Ottoman and Mughal empires immediately come to mind. They encompassed vast territories, commanded rich resources and patronized a variety of talents. The human and material resources that came together under their aegis, particularly in their cities, led to the creation of rich cultural civilizations.

The Mughal empire, founded in the sixteenth century, was one of the richest, most populous and extensive of all time. In its heyday, its political and economic influence was felt far beyond its shores, but more importantly, its cultural impact has reverberated down the centuries, long after the empire itself came to an end. An important part of the legacy of this empire lies in its cities, and of these cities, Shahjahanabad probably best exemplifies the grandeur that came to be associated with the word 'Mughal'. At the same time, it also represented certain other core attributes of the Mughal empire, such as the composite culture that grew on the foundations of the rich cultural diversity of its citizens.

Shahjahanabad came into being at a time when the Mughal empire was at the height of its extent and prosperity, and there was a long tradition of monumental construction behind it. The illustrious ancestor of the Mughals, Timur, had built a grand capital at Samarqand. The Mughals carried to India this Timurid legacy, and married it to the strong local tradition to produce a distinct Mughal style. Architecture in particular flourished under the emperors Akbar and Jahangir, and the best examples were created in Agra and Lahore, which had developed as the principal seats of the empire.

It was at Agra that Shahjahan ascended the throne of his ancestors on 14 February 1628. While his father and grandfather had presided over some remarkable developments in the arts, such as architecture and painting, Shahjahan's particular interest lay in architecture. He commissioned a large number of buildings, and exercised a close personal supervision over the department that was responsible for the execution of building projects. The emperor spent some time every day in the Diwan-e-Khas, his court of special audience, where he consulted with various functionaries to dispose of the business of the empire. An important order of business during these meetings was the examination of designs of buildings, which were laid before him by the architects and superintendents of construction. One of the chief historians of Shahjahan's reign, Adbul Hamid Lahori, wrote: 'The royal mind…pays full attention to the planning and construction…the majority of buildings he designs himself, and on the plans prepared by the skilful architects, after long consideration he makes appropriate alterations and amendations. When the plans have been approved….Asaf Khan [the father of Shahjahan's beloved wife Mumtaz Mahal and, during the early part of Shahjahan's reign, a trusted minister]…writes explanations of the royal orders for the guidance of masons and overseers of buildings.'[1]

The result of this attention to architecture was a spate of construction, particularly in Agra and Lahore. Many of the buildings in the palace complexes of the forts there, which had been built during Akbar and Jahangir's reigns, were pulled down and replaced with newer, grander ones. The crowning glory of the Agra ensemble was the Taj Mahal, the unparalleled mausoleum to Mumtaz Mahal, who died in 1631. This tomb was on a scale more monumental by far than any project till then, and was constructed over a period of twelve years, at the cost of five million rupees. It brought honour, rewards and renown to its architect, Ustad Ahmad.[2]

For Shahjahan, a reworking of the interiors of the fort at Agra did not adequately fulfil his ambitions as a patron of architecture and urban design. The city of Agra, which had grown in a sprawl around the fort, equally did not afford much scope. What was needed was a new city—a truly grand gesture of imperial intent, by which the name of the founder would be remembered. As an eighteenth century history in the Persian language put it: '...exalted emperors always had it in their mind to adorn their reigns with some permanent records, and signalize their times by the establishment of some everlasting landmarks, and consequently this wish was reflected from the mind of Shahjahan in the conception of a city...'[3]

The historian Muhammad Salih, who was an official chronicler of Shahjahan's reign, gave another reason. According to him Agra was a crowded city, with no wide roads. This led to difficulties in the periodic grand processions and assemblies that were part of the emperor's court ritual, as people trying to enter the gates of the fort were crushed.[4]

So, the royal engineers were sent out to find a suitable site for the new city, and they settled on a spot north of Delhi, on the bank of the river Yamuna. The site was just south of the small fort of Salimgarh, built by the Suri ruler Islam Shah in the sixteenth century. Delhi had a long history as a capital of empires. The Delhi Sultanate, which saw the reigns of a succession of rulers—the so-called slave sultans, the Khaljis, Tughlaqs, Syeds and Lodis—for the most part ruled from Delhi. Shahjahan's great-grandfather, Humayun, too, had built a capital city there—Dinpanah, which later came to be called the Purana Qila or 'Old Fort'. Akbar, too, initially ruled from Delhi, building his father's mausoleum there, before making Agra his primary capital. Apart from this aura of royal power, there was a spiritual significance that the city enjoyed. It was the resting place of several prominent Sufi saints. In particular, Delhi contained the shrines of the Chishti saints Qutubuddin Bakhtiyar Kaki, Nizamuddin Auliya and Nasiruddin Chiragh-e-Dehli. These saints were much revered by the Mughals, as they were by both the Muslim and non-Muslim population through much of north India.

What does not figure in the Persian histories of the period, but undoubtedly was a factor in how Delhi was viewed, was its association with Hindu myth and tradition. Ancient tradition associated Delhi with Indraprastha, the holy place where Indra, the king of the Gods, had performed sacrifices and worshipped Vishnu. This spot on the bank of the Yamuna was then blessed by Vishnu, who called it 'Nigambodhak', where a knowledge of the Vedas could be gained simply by taking a dip in the waters.[5] The name 'Nigambodhak' literally meant 'that which makes known the knowledge of the Vedas'. In popular belief, this spot was marked by a place on the banks of the river, called Nigambodh ghat.

In this way, by locating the city in Delhi, and near Nigambodh ghat, Shahjahan was drawing on strong traditions of spiritual and temporal power that the populace associated with the site. By establishing a capital city here, the Mughals could reinforce their legitimacy to rule in the eyes of the people. Delhi was already an important city of the empire.

Even when it had ceased to be the capital after the early part of Akbar's reign, the Mughal emperors had regularly visited Delhi. They did this mainly for three reasons—to visit the shrine of Nizamuddin Auliya, to visit the tomb of Humayun, and to hunt in Palam, which abounded in game, particularly nilgai.

The foundations of the new fort, which was to be the palace complex, were marked out on 29 April 1639. The exact moment was determined by the royal astrologers, and several ceremonies sanctifying the act were also carried out. Needless to say, the plans had been approved by the emperor himself. The foundation stone was laid on 12 May the same year. Skilled artisans from all over the empire gathered to execute the project—stonecutters, sculptors, inlayers, masons, carpenters and many unskilled labourers.[6] There were two architects in charge of the construction of the fort—Ustad Hamid, and Ustad Ahmad. The latter had been the architect of the Taj Mahal. He was also an engineer and learned in astronomy, geometry and mathematics. For his many talents he was honoured by Shahjahan with the title Nadir-al-Asr—'wonder of the age'.[7]

Apart from the architects, a project this complex needed a senior administrator to superintend it. This task was initially entrusted to the then Governor of Delhi province, Ghairat Khan. It then devolved on Illahwardi Khan, the new governor appointed when the former was transferred out of Delhi. By mid-1641, however, the governorship of the province and the superintendence of the project was entrusted to Makramat

Khan, who would carry it to its completion. Makramat Khan, originally from Shiraz in Iran, had migrated to India during the reign of Shahjahan's father, Jahangir. Soon after the accession of Shahjahan, he had been appointed Diwan-e-Buyutat, or 'minister of royal works' and he superintended the construction of the Taj Mahal. Though his job was that of supervising the work, arranging for the materials and coordinating between the emperor and the architects, he was probably well-versed in building techniques. He was also a learned mathematician and astronomer. Moreover he was a close friend of Ustad Ahmad, and the two no doubt worked closely on the construction of Shahjahanabad.[8]

Shahjahan kept himself informed of the progress being made on the palace complex and, from time to time, gave instructions. On a visit to Peshawar in 1646, he saw a covered bazaar that had been constructed there by Ali Mardan Khan, the Governor of Punjab. He admired it and ordered that its plan be immediately sent to Makramat Khan in Delhi, so that it could serve as a model for the covered market, or Chhatta bazaar, in the fort.[9] The emperor also visited the fort while it was under construction. One such visit was on 31 December 1647, when he inspected the buildings and ordered some improvements that occurred to him.[10]

The fort was designed to accommodate the complex administrative machinery of the Mughal capital and the large royal household. It was practically a small self-contained city, containing residences for a large population, buildings for the ceremonial functions of the emperor, and for the administrative and military personnel, workshops for the various crafts produced for the royal household, markets and gardens.

Contemporary observers and court chroniclers have left us detailed accounts of this grand palace complex. It was encircled by a high wall clad in a striking red sandstone, which enclosed a space roughly 820 metres (1000 Shahjahani gaz) long and 492 metres (600 Shahjahani gaz) wide, nearly twice the area of the fort at Agra.[11] The fort was surrounded on three sides by a moat 8.2 metres (10 gaz) deep and 20.5 metres (25 gaz) broad, and on the eastern side it adjoined the river. Beside the moat were gardens with colourful flowers. The red wall surrounding the palace complex would in later years give the complex its popular name—Red Fort.

The encircling wall of the Red Fort was pierced by two prominent gates. One of these was located to the west and was

The Lahore Gate of the Red Fort. A newspaper illustration from 1857.

known as Lahori Darwaza because it opened in the direction of Lahore. The other major entrance was to the south, and was known as Dilli Darwaza or Akbarabadi Darwaza, because it opened in the direction of the south where lay the older cities of Delhi and also Akbarabad (the Mughal name for Agra). This gate was flanked by two large stone sculptures of elephants, and due to this was also known as Hatiapol (elephant gate).

There were four other, less prominent, openings—one linking the fort to Salimgarh, one giving access from the emperor's own quarters to the river, and two others, also opening to the river. Despite the battlemented walls and the moat, the palace complex was not a heavily fortified structure. Located at the heart of the Mughal empire, away from vulnerable frontier areas, it was not really designed to withstand heavy attacks.

The interior of the palace complex was laid out in a pleasing symmetry. The grand palace buildings were strung out in a row along the eastern perimeter of the fort, on a raised terrace. There were no battlements on this side of the fort, and the buildings commanded a view of the river, which flowed at the foot of the fort wall, separated from it by a wide sandy bank. The buildings on the riverfront included the Diwan-e-Khas (the emperor's more exclusive court of audience), the Aramgah (his personal chamber), the Imtiyaz Mahal (the main palace of the emperor), and several other palace buildings, including the palace of his eldest and favourite daughter Jahanara—who enjoyed the title Begum Sahiba.[12] These buildings were richly decorated with marble carved and inlaid with semi-precious stones, painted and moulded plaster, and mirror work. Almost all of the major riverfront buildings were designed as open pavilions, lightly screened by pierced marble screens on the side that faced the river. Deep awnings and draperies that changed with the seasons gave protection against the elements. On the western side, each was fronted by a walled courtyard, which gave it privacy from the rest of the fort. Pools and gardens filled the courtyards of these private palaces.

Through these palaces on the riverfront ran a shallow channel of water from the north towards the south, widening in places to form pools, and cascading in a waterfall before the Imtiyaz Mahal. This channel was an offshoot of a canal, part of which had been constructed in the fourteenth century by the emperor Firoz Shah Tughlaq, to bring water from the Yamuna to his hunting preserve at Safidon (in the present-day state of Haryana). This was now repaired and extended to supply water to the city as well as the palace, and was called the Nahar-e-bahisht, 'stream of paradise'.

The Mughal love for symmetry in architecture was reflected not only in the orderly rectangular forms of the buildings, but also in the layout of the thoroughfares within the fort. Of these, none was more important than the imperial axis, which ran east to west through the middle of the fort, linking the emperor's palace and court in a straight line with the main street of the city. This axis had a very formal layout, and emphasized the grandeur associated with the court and palace of the emperor. At one end of this axis was the Imtiyaz Mahal, the main royal palace. From the secluded garden of this palace, the emperor entered through a private doorway into the Diwan-e-Khas-o-Aam (also called the Diwan-e-Aam)—the general court of audience where he would hold his big durbars or royal assemblages. This was a large building with the throne placed on a high platform under a marble canopy. Next along this axis was the Naqqar Khana, or drum house, where ceremonial music was played as part of the royal panoply. The large forecourt in front of this building was a hub where two major paths intersected. This forecourt led into the covered market that extended to the Lahori Gate.

The other important axis, which intersected with the east-west axis at the forecourt in front of the Naqqar Khana, came from the Dilli Darwaza, and then led further north. Its northern section led to the stables, and the southern section was lined with shops. In the middle of this street flowed a channel of water.

The fort included a variety of other structures and spaces. In the north-eastern quadrant there were two large gardens—the Mahtab Bagh, and the Hayat Baksh Bagh. Both had channels of water, a variety of trees and parterres planted with colourful flowers. The Mughals were very interested in horticultural pursuits, and some rare plants were grown in the gardens in the fort. The Hayat Baksh Bagh had two beautiful pavilions, built of carved and inlaid marble, named Sawan and Bhadon, after the two rainy months of the Indian calendar. On one side of the latter garden, close to the Diwan-e-Khas, was the Hammam. This was the elaborate royal bath, designed with cold and hot baths, a steam room and a perfumed changing room. As the only part of the royal buildings that was not richly carpeted, it had a floor profusely inlaid with semi-precious stones.

The south-eastern quarter of the fort contained the residences of the extended Mughal family, and in the coming centuries it would get increasingly more densely built up, as the numbers of those living there increased. The western part of the fort was less formally laid out, and was occupied by the administrative, military and manufacturing departments and personnel.

The construction of the fort was completed in just over nine years, at a cost of some six million rupees.[13] The formal inauguration was a grand affair, expressed in opulence, ceremony and ritual. The royal astrologers prescribed the auspicious time, on 6 April 1648, when the emperor would leave Agra to come to Delhi. He covered the distance for the most part overland, but the last stretch was completed by boat. The emperor alighted on the riverbank and entered his palace through his royal entrance on 18 April at the precise moment determined by the astrologers. After a tour of all the buildings, the emperor sat on a jewelled throne in the Diwan-e-Khas-o-Aam, and held a darbar amidst the ceremonial beating of drums and playing of shehnais. A vast canopy, covering some 3,200 square yards, under which ten thousand men could stand, was set up in the courtyard of the Diwan-e-Khas-o-Aam. It had been specially manufactured in Gujarat, embellished with gold embroidery and supported on silver columns.

The completion of the fort, which also marked the formal

founding of the new city, was marked by court poets with appropriate verses of praise. Mir Yahiya Kashi composed a chronogram to mark the date. Chronograms were widely used mnemonic devices, which worked on the principle that each letter of the alphabet was accorded a numerical value. Thus, words and phrases could be put together in a way that would yield a desired number, corresponding to a date, or more correctly, a year. Yahiya Kashi's chronogram read: *shud Shahjahanabad az Shahjahan abad* (Shahjahan founded Shahjahanabad) which yields the year 1058 according to the Hijri era which was then in use. In terms of the common era used today, this corresponds to 1648. The poet was rewarded with a gift of 5,000 rupees.[14]

The celebrations lasted for ten days, during which rich gifts were offered by important noblemen of the empire to the emperor. The emperor in turn bestowed honours, titles, promotions and gifts on several members of the royal family, and on important officials. Prince Dara Shukoh—the eldest and favourite son of Shahjahan, received a three-fold increase in his mansab or rank, and Jahanara received a gift of 400,000 rupees. Those who had been associated with the construction of the fort were recognized. Makramat Khan was awarded an increase in his mansab, and the numerous artisans were given gifts of money. Towards the end of the celebrations, Shahjahan's fifty-eighth birthday according to the lunar calendar, was celebrated.[15] An important part of the birthday celebrations was the Mughal custom of weighing the emperor against different items, such as gold, silver, precious stones, coins, grain and salt. These were then distributed in charity.[16]

While the construction of the fort was on, it occupied the entire attention of the imperial works department, and no other projects were undertaken in the surrounding city. After the fort was complete, however, certain other projects were undertaken. One was the city wall. A wall of earth and stones was put up in a short period of four months in 1650, but since it collapsed in the monsoon the following year, a more permanent wall was ordered to be built. This wall, made of stone and mortar, and punctuated by several entrances, was completed in 1657, at a cost of 500,000 rupees.[17] It was not a great defensive structure, and contemporary European visitors such as the Frenchman Francois Bernier, who visited the city in 1660, did not think highly of it. In a letter to a friend, Bernier described the fortifications as being very inadequate. There was no moat, there were a few bastions, and there was just a bank of earth four or five feet thick, on the inside.[18] No doubt given the position of the capital at the heart of the empire, it was never imagined that strong defences would be required.

Broad streets were laid out in the city, closely mirroring the symmetry within the fort. The east-west axis was an extension of the imperial axis that linked the Lahori Gate to the Imtiyaz Mahal. This was a long and wide street, with a channel of water running down its middle, and trees providing shade. It was lined on both sides with arcaded shops. These arcades had flat terrace roofs, behind which were the residences of the shopkeepers. The street was divided into three sections by two large squares. The first section of the street, from the fort to the first square, was called Urdu Bazaar—the bazaar of the royal camp. It got its name from its proximity to the square in front of the fort, where many troops patrolled. This bazaar terminated in the Kotwali Chowk, the square named after the police station, the kotwali, that stood there.

From the Kotwali Chowk onwards, the street was called Asharfi Bazaar, literally the 'money market'. This ended at a large octagonal square, called Chandni Chowk. This space had been commissioned by the princess Jahanara. Jahanara was a very wealthy woman. On her mother's death in 1631 she had inherited property worth more than five million rupees, which was half of her mother's fortune, the other half being divided among her siblings. In addition to this, in 1644 she had been given the revenues of the province and the flourishing fort of Surat, which amounted annually to over one million rupees.[19]

The chowk had a large pool in its centre, reflecting the moonlight, or chandni, which gave the square its name. To the south of this square was a hammam, or public bath, also commissioned by the princess. To the north of the square lay a two-storied sarai or inn, built on the orders of Jahanara. On the other, northern side of this sarai lay a vast garden. This garden had been laid out by Makramat Khan, and was presented by Shahjahan to Jahanara. It came to be known as Bagh Sahibabad, after her title, Begum Sahiba.[20] Through the garden ran the Nahar-e-bahisht, the same channel of water from the Yamuna that later entered the Red Fort, and passed through the large gardens which lay along the same axis as this one. To the west of Chandni Chowk lay the Fathepuri Bazaar, terminating in the Fatehpuri mosque, built by Fatehpuri Begum, a wife of Shahjahan.

Another great street in the city was the extension of the main north-south axis within the fort, which led from the Naqqar Khana to the Akbarabadi Gate. This street, which was called Faiz Bazaar, connected the latter gate to the southern gate of the city, also known as the Akbarabadi or Delhi Gate. This street, too, was lined with shops, and had a channel of water running down its middle.

A little over a year after the completion of the palace complex, the imperial builders started work on another monumental project—the Jama Masjid or congregational mosque. Its foundations were laid in 1650 and it was completed in 1656. The royal chronicler Mohammad Salih Kanbo has noted that Sa'adullah Khan, a trusted noble of Shahjahan, and Khalil Ullah Khan (appointed governor of Delhi in 1653) supervised the construction.[21] The architect of the Red Fort, Ustad Ahmad, had died in 1649, but it is possible that he worked on the early stages of the design. His son, Nurullah, was the calligrapher who designed the inscriptions on the mosque.[22] This large mosque was built on a natural height in the land, and was the largest mosque in the Mughal empire. A wide street, called Khas bazaar, linked its large eastern gate to the Akbarabadi Gate of the fort. Halfway between the mosque and the fort was a square known as Chowk Sa'adullah Khan. A college and a hospital were also built in the square surrounding the mosque.[23]

All the important mosques in the city were built by members of the royal family. Somewhat to the west of Fatehpuri mosque, which has already been mentioned as having been built by Fatehpuri Begum, was Sirhindi Masjid, built by Sirhindi Begum. At the northern end of Faiz Bazar was the Akbarabadi Masjid, built by Akbarabadi Begum. All these ladies were wives of Shahjahan, and were known by appellations that referred to the towns where they came from, instead of having their personal names taken in public.

There were two other imperial projects that were undertaken, outside the walls of the city. Both were large gardens. One, some seven to eight kilometres to the north-west, was founded by royal order, and then gifted by the

Jama Masjid, painted by the famous uncle-nephew team of Thomas and William Daniell. Published in 1795.

emperor to Akbarabadi Begum. The garden was completed at a cost of a million rupees, and the lady had also added to it a sarai. This garden was named Bagh A'izzabad (precious garden) but in later years came to be known also as Aghrabad and Shalimar.[24] The other was a garden known as Roshanara Bagh, located just over a kilometre to the north-west of the city. It was named after it patron Roshanara Begum, the younger sister of Jahanara.

The palace complex, the city wall, the grand bazaar streets with their squares, the imperial mosques and gardens, were important landmarks of the city. All the other spaces were filled in by individual enterprise. As the city took shape, the nobility began building their own homes in the new capital. The emperor's favourite son, Dara Shukoh, built a large mansion north of the fort, at the then princely sum of 400,000 rupees.[25] Similarly, mansions were built by the wazir or chief minister, Shaista Khan (who was also the brother of Mumtaz Mahal), Ali Mardan Khan, Shidi Miftah, the African-Indian noble, and Ustad Hamid, one of the architects of the Red Fort.[26]

These mansions stood within generous compounds amidst gardens with water channels and fountains. The interiors were decorated with painted ceilings and walls with niches containing porcelain vases. The floors were spread with mattresses and cushions to sit on, covered with finely embroidered or brocade silks. The houses included underground chambers to which the family would retire to escape from the heat of summer. The compounds in which these mansions were set also contained the large households of these grandees—including the extended family of the owners, many domestic retainers, troops, etc. There were also, of course, many smaller homes.[27] Those of the shopkeepers above or behind their shops in bazaar streets have already been mentioned.

Some of the neighbourhoods of the city pre-dated the foundation of Shahjahanabad. The city had not been established on completely empty land; rather, it absorbed existing structures and road alignments within its precincts. There was an important diagonal street, leading from the north-west to the south-east, which was actually a pre-existing road flanked by many older structures. These included the shrine of Shah Turkman, the Sufi saint who died in 1240, and near whose shrine Delhi's only woman ruler, Razia Sultan, had been buried in 1242. The city gate closest to this was named Turkman Darwaza. On this road were situated a few mosques dating to the fourteenth century, including the important Kalan Masjid, built by Khan-e-Jahan, the minister of Firoz Shah Tughlaq. Since it had been a highway, wells had also been built along this road, particularly during the reign of Sher Shah Suri, in the sixteenth century. This included the red sandstone well known as Lal Kuan, as well as the stepwell that turned brackish and was therefore called Khari Baoli. The banks of the river had also been used before the city was founded. Nigambodh ghat, with steps leading down to the river, had been used by Hindus for bathing, and continued to be so used once Shahjahanabad was founded. The ghats to the south of the Red Fort were where boats, carrying grains and other merchandise that was transported on the river, were unloaded. The market beside these ghats, where the goods were traded, was called Daryaganj. With the foundation of Shahjahanabad, this was incorporated within the walls of the city.

In the course of time many different neighbourhoods, or mohallas, grew within the city, not dictated by imperial planning, but based on the needs of the people. Many artisans lived and worked in close proximity to others of the same trade. They thus formed the nuclei of neighbourhoods that drew their names and identity from these occupational groups. Some of these mohallas, which also went by the name of katras (commercial enclaves) or kuchas (lanes), included Katra

A jewellers' workshop in Dariba, painted by William Simpson, 1867.

Nil (named after indigo dyers), Churiwalan (bangle makers), Chipiwara (fabric printers), Dhobiwara, Dhobiyan and Dhobi ka Katra (washermen), Namdewalan (felt makers), Rodgaran (tallow makers), Qassabpura (butchers), Kucha Nechabandon ka (huqqa tube makers) and several others.

One neighbourhood that owed its origin and occupational structure specifically to an imperial decision was Dariba, which was inhabited by Jain merchants. The Jains had been the bankers of empires for centuries. The Sultanate rulers who preceded the Mughals, as well as the Mughal emperors, gave important positions to Jain bankers and merchants in their financial departments. So when Shahjahan established his new capital, he invited Dipchand Sah, a well-known Aggarwal Jain merchant of Hisar, to set up his business in Shahjahanabad. The merchant was allotted a large amount of land quite close to the Red Fort, where he is believed to have built havelis or mansions for his sixteen sons. Following from this, a major Jain temple was built in front of the Lahore Gate of the Red Fort (this is today called the Digambar Jain Lal Mandir), and another was built near the Delhi Gate of the city.[28]

There has been much debate about the nature of Shahjahanabad, and where it fits into different models of urbanization—was it an 'Islamic City', or a 'Sovereign City'—the capital of a 'patrimonial-bureaucratic empire' where all power flowed from the emperor? Or was it a typically Indian construct, the product of a syncretic culture based on an intermingling of people?[29] Probably it might be right to characterize it as a typically Mughal city, representing all that the Mughal empire stood for.

In the mid-seventeenth century, when the city was founded, the Mughal empire certainly stood for grandeur, and for the aura of majesty surrounding the persona of the Mughal emperor. Many features in the basic structure of the palace and city were designed to showcase this majesty. In the Aramgah, the emperor's personal chamber (known more popularly now as the Khwabgah), there was a projecting window surmounted by a gilded dome, known as the Jharokha-e-Darshan. As the name of this implied, it was the window where the emperor gave 'darshan' to his subjects gathered on the sandy bank of the river below. The concept of darshan or 'viewing' was usually applied in the Hindu tradition to deities, and worshippers catching a glimpse of the deity were believed to be blessed by the act.

The grand imperial courts—the Diwan-e-Aam and the Diwan-e-Khas, were designed to enable the large durbars or assemblies that were a part of Mughal court practice. The magnificence of their embellishments—the gold painting, the inlays of precious stones, the rich carpets and draperies, all generally conveyed the opulence of the empire. In addition, some motifs carried a deeper symbolism. The Aramgah, where the emperor conducted the business of the empire with his closest ministers, was decorated with carvings of the scales of justice, symbolizing the justice of the emperor; and with carvings of the sun, representing his luminous majesty.

The wall behind the high throne canopy in the Diwan-e-Aam was decorated with an unusual allegorical theme. The centerpiece was a small inlaid panel, imported from Italy. In Europe, such panels were typically set into cabinets and other furniture. They also formed part of the goods imported into the Mughal empire and found their way into royal collections. This particular panel shows an image common in European classicism—that of the mythical Greek poet and singer, Orpheus, surrounded by animals that he has charmed through his music. Surrounding this panel are many others, showing various birds and animals. Why was this composition chosen for such an important position, framing the emperor seated on his throne?

The depiction of animals—predator and prey together—was in fact a common allegorical theme in Mughal painting. It symbolized the overarching justice and protection of the emperor, under which the oppressed were shielded from the oppressors, and all lived together in peace and harmony. Through the placement of these images, this message was sought to be reinforced in the minds of all who attended the court of the emperor.[30]

Even in the city outside the fort walls, the stage was set to represent the grandeur of the emperor. The broad main streets were designed to enable impressive processions. As the emperor went to pray at the Jama Masjid, or as he left the city to the north or to the south, his magnificent procession of elephants, horses, palanquins and carriages made an impressive spectacle.

The alignment of the main streets of the city with those in the palace symbolically strengthened the connection of the emperor with his subjects living outside the walls of the palace complex. This connection was symbolically carried forward outside the city too. The streets led to the gates, which gave access to the highways. The naming of the several gates of the city after the far-flung provinces of the empire—Kashmir, Agra, Lahore, Kabul, Ajmer—symbolically represented the capital as the heart of the empire, linked to its limbs by these arteries.

Within the city, freedom was given to various groups to set up their places of work and residence. Large mansions were interspersed with more modest dwellings, and groups of different ethnic and religious affiliations were represented. All of this reflected the heterogeneity and harmony, expressed best in Akbar's policy of Sulh-e-Kul (peace with all), which was the ideal that the Mughal empire aspired to.

A view of the city of Shahjahanabad, from the Red Fort.
Drawn by Alexis Soltykoff, 1840s.

The Imperial Capital

THE INAUGURATION OF THE NEW CAPITAL, HERALDED BY THE
arrival of the emperor's court, brought new life to the city that
had been designed with much care and deliberation. Delhi
had, of course, already been a major city of North India, a
thriving trade and manufacturing centre. Now it had become
the residence of the emperor, his extended family and large
household, together with the ministers and courtiers who

also made Shahjahanabad their home. This brought a new level of patronage, culture and commerce to the city. In the mid-seventeenth century the population is believed to have been around 600,000; greater than Paris, which was the most populous city of Western Europe at the time.[31]

The emperor did not stay in the capital all the time. In order to keep effective control over a farflung empire, the ruler needed to travel, often to distant provinces. And since in those days such travel took considerable time, he would often base himself there for a while. So, barely seven months after the inauguration, Shahjahan left for Lahore, only to return in January 1650, a year and two months later. This was a pattern that continued for the rest of Shahjahan's reign. He left again in February 1651 for Kashmir, and returned in December 1652. In December 1653 he left for Agra, and came back to the capital in January 1654. In the winter later that year, he again left for a three-month absence, to visit Ajmer, and for a two-month trip in the first half of 1657, to a newly constructed retreat in Mukhlispur (near Muzaffarabad, in present day Uttar Pradesh).[32]

Though the emperor spent almost as much time outside Shahjahanabad as he spent in it, when he was there, the residents certainly were aware of his presence. One evidence of his presence was aural—every day, at fixed times, loud music from the Naqqar Khana would sound, and those living in the neighbourhood of the fort could hear it. Francois Bernier, who spent a considerable time in Delhi, described how lying in bed at night, the sound of the 'solemn, grand and melodious' music reached his ears from afar.[33]

Then, those going to the bathing ghats on the river at dawn could have a darshan of their emperor, who would sit in the Jharokha-e-Darshan for an hour or an hour-and-a-half. The court historian, Abdul Hamid Lahori, gave two explanations for why the practice of darshan had been adopted by the Mughal emperors. One was 'to enable His Majesty's subjects to witness the simultaneous appearance of the sky-adorning sun and the world-conquering Emperor, and thereby receive without any obstacle or hindrance the blessing of both these luminaries'. This, clearly, was with the purpose of enhancing the aura of the emperor and forging an emotional link with his subjects. A later historian, Khafi Khan, spoke of some Hindus being called 'darshani'—'for until they had seen the person of the King at the window, they put not a morsel of food into their mouths'. But there was a more practical purpose too, as Abdul Hamid went on to explain. The people who gathered on the sand bank below the Jharokha also got an opportunity to put forward their petitions and grievances directly before the emperor. Officials who were present at the time would immediately make a note of the case and later lay it before the emperor in the presence of his ministers in the halls of public or private audience.[34]

A glimpse of the emperor could also be had as he went in procession on Fridays to the Jama Masjid, to join in congregational worship. The emperor's first such visit to the mosque was on the occasion of Eid-ul-Fitr, in July 1656, shortly after the construction of the mosque had been completed. On this occasion, the entire route, from the front of the Naqqar Khana inside the fort, to the mosque, 'was flanked by two rows of elephants with gold and silver housings, besides a great many musketeers, matchlock and rocketmen.' On Eid-ul-Zuha, the emperor used to go to the Eidgah, constructed outside the city walls in 1655.[35]

The residence of the royal family in the capital also led to other occasional spectacles. On the bank of the river below the palace walls, elephant fights sometimes took place—with the royal family watching from their palace windows, while the populace would throng the bank below. In April 1654, Sulaiman Shukoh, the son of Dara Shukoh, was married to a young woman who was the granddaughter of Raja Gaj Singh of Marwar, and great-niece of Raja Jai Singh of Amer. On that occasion a bright spectacle was organized on the riverside. A mock fort was constructed out of timber, with towers at regular intervals on which lamps were placed. The whole place was also lit with a fireworks display.[36]

The closest encounter with the true grandeur of the Mughal emperor that a relatively ordinary individual could have, was attendance at the durbar or public audience. This was held in the Diwan-e-Khas-o-Aam, and detailed accounts have been left behind, particularly by foreign visitors such as the Venetian, Niccolao Manucci. The emperor sat on his elevated throne balcony, which was surrounded by a low golden railing. The only courtiers allowed within this railing were his own sons, and of these, only Dara Shukoh was allowed to sit. Several feet below, in the large pillared hall surrounded by a silver railing, stood ministers, officials and other important functionaries. Outside the hall, within a red sandstone railing, stood those of a lower rank. Just outside this railing, in the large courtyard, stood nine horses on either side, and beyond them, a total of four elephants with decorative trappings. Many armed soldiers stood guard in this courtyard.

Despite this large gathering of men and beasts, the visitor was struck by the complete silence, except for the ceremonial music played in the Naqqar Khana to announce the arrival of His Majesty. Order and decorum were maintained by special functionaries, carrying gold or silver sticks. Manucci, who was presented by a court official to the emperor, only made his obeisance from outside the silver railing, bowing down low and touching the back of his hand to the ground and raising it to his forehead—repeating the gesture three times, as he had practiced beforehand.[37] Apart from the regular durbars, there were periodic celebrations, such as the emperor's solar and lunar birthdays, the anniversary of his accession to the throne, Eid, and Nauroz—the Persian new year. These were celebrated with gifts for the emperor, and honours and promotions for his courtiers.

An example of the favours given out during such occasions can be found in the official report of the first Nauroz celebrated by Shahjahan in his new capital. We are told that 'Imperial warrants were also issued, summoning to court many of the grandees and nobles who were away at their jagirs and homes'. Important ministers and jagirdars, such as Ali Mardan Khan, Sa'adullah Khan, Raja Jaswant Singh (who succeeded Gaj Singh as ruler of Marwar), Raja Jai Singh and numerous others were accorded robes of honour. Jahanara gifted her father jewels and clothes worth 100,000 rupees, and was in turn awarded the revenues of the pargana of Panipat, which amounted to some 2,50,000 rupees annually. Fatehpuri Begum and Akbarabadi Begum each received 100,000 rupees.[38]

Very occasionally, the dignity of the court could be disrupted, causing a sensation, as happened on the occasion of the emperor's sixty-fourth lunar birthday in 1654. An important part of the celebrations, which took place in the Diwan-e-Khas-o-Aam, was the weighing of the emperor. For this he descended from the balcony on which he usually sat, and came to a jewelled throne placed in the centre of the hall. At this point one of the officials, Jasrup Mirathia, who was standing outside the silver railing, rushed at him with a

The Diwan-e-Khas, in a drawing from the mid-nineteenth century.

drawn sword. He had hardly gone a step or two however, when Naubat Khan, the kotwal (the head of police), struck him down with the truncheon he was holding. Jasrup was also stabbed by other bystanders.[39]

The Diwan-e-Khas-o-Aam was not just reserved for grand audiences with the emperor. There was at least one particular kind of occasion on which it was put to public use. In 1650, Shahjahan completed sixty years of age according to the lunar calendar. According to Islamic law, he was now exempt from keeping the fast during the holy month of Ramzan, in lieu of charity. Apart from distributing sixty thousand rupees to the poor, the emperor ordered that every night through the month, a feast would be laid out for the poor in the hall of the Diwan-e-Khas-o-Aam. Thenceforth, this became an annual feature of Shahjahan's reign.[40]

Manucci saw Delhi and the imperial court as a seventeen-year-old in 1656, recently arrived in India and Delhi. He found there a relatively large community of Europeans, several of whom were employed in the royal artillery, and others who were surgeons. He himself entered the service of Dara Shukoh's artillery at a salary of eighty rupees per month, which, within two years, had risen to one hundred and fifty rupees. This was a generous salary and the European artillerymen were a pampered lot. As Manucci put it, 'European artillerymen who took service in that branch had only to take aim; as for all the rest—the fatigue of raising, lowering, loading, and firing—this was the business of artificers or labourers kept for the purpose.' With little work and a good pay, these Europeans soon became known for their drunkenness and bad behaviour. The drunkenness was encouraged by the fact that Europeans employed by Dara were allowed to distill and sell alcoholic spirits. Manucci soon entered into an illegal partnership with a man who used him as a front for his enterprise, paying him ten rupees per month for the privilege.[41]

Delhi was a melting pot of communities and cultures. The Mughal army and bureaucracy themselves afforded avenues for employment, which attracted talent from far and wide. Turanis from Transoxiana (the area now covered by Uzbekistan, Tajikistan, southern Kyrgyzstan and south-west Kazakhstan), and Afghans were primarily men of arms, while the Iranis were men of letters. The Firangis (the term applied to all Europeans) were usually employed as artillerymen or doctors and surgeons. We also find mention of European women who were surgeons. Arabs, Habshis (Africans) and Rumis (from parts of the Turkish empire) were often in the armed forces. The post of the kotwal at Delhi was frequently occupied by a Habshi. Apart from these relative newcomers, there was, of course, a large number of people from India or those who had lived in India for many generations. These included Muslims as well as Hindus—Rajput and Jat armed men; Khatris, Aggarwals, Kayasths and Kashmiris in the bureaucracy.[42]

For European expatriates such as Manucci and Bernier, everything they saw was new and therefore interesting. They have, therefore, left behind frank and detailed accounts of the city and the court. They, however, also picked up a lot of bazaar gossip, which found itself into their accounts. Manucci, for instance, wrote at length of Shahjahan's supposed sexual promiscuousness, and of his daughters' alleged dalliance with a series of lovers, and Bernier further embroidered this with fantastic anecdotes. One of the most notorious and improbable of these was the story of how Jahanara, on one occasion, surprised by the sudden arrival of her father, hid a lover in a large cauldron. Shahjahan however suspected the truth, and ordered a fire lit under it, and stood there until he was sure that the man inside was dead, with the princess, meanwhile, keeping a stiff upper lip.[43]

European observers however often laboured under misapprehensions born of their ignorance of local customs as well as their prejudices. One example is Manucci's description of the women's bazaar held in the palace during Shahjahan's reign. This was an eight-day gala, where women of the palace and the city put up stalls, where they sold handicrafts, fabrics, jewels and other merchandise. To Manucci this was an excuse for the emperor to see and take his pick from among the women of the city, as 'no one was allowed to enter except women'. This was clearly a very prejudiced view of a particular social situation. The fair, or more properly a women's market, called Meena Bazaar, was, in fact, for the benefit of the ladies of the palace, who lived in seclusion, shielded from the eyes of strange men. It gave the purveyors of goods from the city an opportunity to display their wares to them, as well as allowing the numerous women inside the palace to sell their own wares.[44]

European observers invariably commented on the large number of women inside the palace complex. Their presence is easily explained. With no strange men allowed to invade the privacy of the women's quarters, all functions were performed by women. They were the armed guards, palanquin-bearers, messengers, secretaries, as well as domestic workers. One of the women employed in the palace, in charge of the royal table, was a Portuguese lady called Thomazia Martins, whose husband was a soldier in the army.[45]

The inauguration of the new capital brought a greater prosperity to the city. The presence of the court created a market for luxury goods, and made the city an even greater destination than it had been for rich merchants from Iran and Central Asia, most of whom would stop at Jahanara's sarai.[46] The markets were full of goods from distant lands, including expensive exotic fruits like apples, pears, grapes and melons, and dry fruits and nuts, such as raisins, prunes, apricots, almonds, pistachios and walnuts from Uzbekistan and Iran.[47]

The presence of troops and their officers provided a market for a somewhat different variety of goods and services. In front of the gates of the Red Fort, where the two main streets of the city met, was the Chowk Sa'adullah Khan. In this square were the troops of the Rajas whose turn it was to periodically mount the guard. This led to the development of a bazaar and public space, to which came a number of jugglers, storytellers and astrologers.[48] Entertainment was also provided by an important social group in the city—that of the kanchanis, or singing and dancing women. These were recognized as professionals by the state and taxed. Some of them were very wealthy women, paid handsomely when they went to perform at the homes of the wealthy or even at the palace. Some earned good money from giving public performances in the city, in open spaces lit by torches, from six to nine at night.[49]

Defining the urbanity and cosmopolitanism of the city was the example set by Dara Shukoh. The prince had been declared the heir apparent by Shahjahan and enjoyed great influence and wealth through the generous affection of his father. The prince had an intellectual, even mystical, bent of mind and was open to new ideas and people. He spent considerable time in the company of learned men of all faiths and persuasions. He included among his friends the Flemish Jesuit priest, Father Busee, as well as Sarmad, an Armenian Jew who had converted to Islam and adopted unorthodox beliefs and an extremely ascetic lifestyle, which included giving up wearing clothes. Dara also regularly consulted the astrologer Bhawani Das.[50]

Dara Shukoh's years in Shahjahanabad were particularly productive for him in terms of intellectual output. His efforts to make a study of Hindu scriptures with the help of learned men of that faith led to his writing two important works. One, completed in 1655, was the *Majma-ul-Bahrain* ('The mingling of the two oceans'). In this Dara sought to trace parallels between Sufism and Vedanta, coming to the conclusion that 'there were not many differences, except verbal, in the ways in which Hindu monotheists and Muslim Sufis sought and comprehended truth.' In 1657 he completed a translation of the Upanishads into Persian.[51]

Less than ten years after the inauguration of the capital, there was a crisis that threw the capital, as well as the empire, into turmoil. On 16 September 1657, Shahjahan fell seriously ill. As he appeared neither in court nor at the Jharokha-e-Darshan, soon rumours started circulating that the emperor was at death's door, or even that he was dead. There was great unease among people in the city who anticipated anarchy and disorder. For three days, shops were closed and there was a dearth of supplies. The bankers sent news to other parts of the country through their network of couriers, that the emperor was already dead. The three sons of Shahjahan—Aurangzeb, Shuja and Murad—who were in distant provinces, received similar news from their agents at the court.[52]

By 24 September the emperor was somehow able to manage an appearance at the Jharokha-e-Darshan, to reassure the people that he was still alive. To further convince people that he was well on the road to recovery, zakat taxes of Shahjahanabad district to the tune of 750,000 rupees were remitted 'in celebration of the emperor's improvement'. However the emperor was far from well, and Dara Shukoh was entrusted with much of the management of affairs of state, at the same time as his nomination as the successor was confirmed.[53]

By the end of October, Shahjahan had recovered enough to set out on a journey to Agra, hoping that the change of air would do him good. In the meanwhile, however, civil war was brewing, and the empire soon erupted in a contest for power between the four princes. In this, Aurangzeb was soon able to gain the upper hand. He comprehensively defeated the forces of Dara Shukoh at the battle of Samugarh in June 1658. With Dara on the run, Aurangzeb immediately laid siege to the fort of Agra, forcing its surrender and imprisoning his father in the palace, where the latter was eventually to die on 31 January 1666. Having imprisoned Shahjahan, Aurangzeb returned to Shahjahanabad. Murad Baksh, who had been on Aurangzeb's side in Samugarh but was deemed to have independent ambitions, was imprisoned. He was kept for a while in Salimgarh in Delhi, then in Gwalior, where he was executed in 1661. In Shahjahanabad, on 31 July 1658, suggested by the astrologers as an auspicious date, Aurangzeb assumed the crown of his ancestors. The ceremony took place, not in the Red Fort, but in Shalimar Bagh.[54] Though by this time Shahjahan and Murad Baksh had been imprisoned, Shah Shuja and Dara Shukoh were still at large. Maybe that is why the new emperor did not feel confident enough to proclaim his accession within the walls of Shahjahanabad.

The pursuit of the other two princes continued; Shah Shuja was defeated at the battle of Khajua in January 1659, and eventually disappeared into Arakan, never to be heard from again. Dara Shukoh was pursued westward by the imperial forces, and suffered successive defeats until he was left with a very small contingent. Finally in June 1659, in Sindh, the zamindar of Dadhar, Malik Jiwan, treacherously captured him and handed him over to Aurangzeb's generals. A few days before this, confident that he had vanquished his enemies, Aurangzeb celebrated a second coronation ceremony. This was held in the Diwan-e-Khas-o-Aam on 15 June 1659, where Aurangzeb sat on the famous Peacock Throne, adorned with fabulous jewels, that had been commissioned by his father.[55]

Dara Shukoh and his son, Sipihr Shukoh, were brought to Delhi in September, and were subjected to public humiliation on the orders of the emperor. Shabbily dressed in tattered clothes and with their feet chained, they were seated on an elephant and paraded through the streets of the city. The sight of the prince sitting abjectly with bowed head in the open howdah moved the crowd that had gathered, and there was a public outcry.[56]

Malik Jiwan, who had handed over Dara and his family to their enemies, was honoured with rewards and titles, but the people of Delhi demonstrated their strong disapproval of the role he had played. When he entered the city two days after Dara had been paraded through the streets, he and his party were set upon by a mob, and, 'assailing Jiwan and his companions with abuse and imprecations, they pelted them with dirt and filth, and clods and stones, so that several persons were knocked down and killed, and many were wounded'. People standing on the roofs of their houses threw excrement and ashes from pots on their heads, and Jiwan Khan barely escaped with his life into the palace. The atmosphere in the city that day verged on rebellion, only just kept in check by the kotwal and his policemen.[57]

Despite this strong public opinion in Delhi, Aurangzeb remained firm in his determination to wipe out his brother. For some days Dara was kept prisoner in the garden of Khizrabad, some miles to the south of Shahjahanabad. Meanwhile, legal opinions were obtained that justified his being put to death on charges of apostasy and heresy. He was executed and his head brought for inspection by Aurangzeb, who then ordered that the body be paraded once more through the streets before being buried in the tomb of Humayun.[58] Some months later, Sarmad, who had been close to Dara Shukoh and scornful of Aurangzeb's authority, was also held guilty of blasphemy and executed.[59]

The death of Dara Shukoh and the exile of Shahjahan brought an end to the civil war, but the miseries of the people were not over. The disorders of war had been combined with a drought, which had destroyed crops and led to an acute shortage of foodgrains. This led to an influx of the starving poor into Shahjahanabad from the badly affected districts, and large numbers came and camped in the streets and bazaars of the city. Many took refuge in the area surrounding the city, which was dotted with tombs and ruins of earlier cities. By imperial order ten langar khanas, or free kitchens, were set up within the city walls, and twelve outside, to provide food to this starving population. These were in addition to existing free kitchens that used to distribute raw and cooked food to the poor. Many taxes, particularly those on the sale and transport of grain, were remitted or abolished altogether, to bring down prices.[60]

Some years into the reign of Aurangzeb, certain fundamental changes came about in the social life of the city. Aurangzeb was of a puritanical bent of mind, and set about correcting what he thought of as a moral laxity that had set into society in the capital. Measures were taken to ban the consumption of alcohol and intoxicants, and to shut down taverns and brothels. Though Christians are said to have still been permitted to brew alcohol, these activities were shifted to the suburbs and sale was prohibited.[61] A spate of reforms came in 1668. Prohibitions were placed on singing and dancing as occupations, and the court's patronage to these artists was also discontinued. Those whose occupations were hit by these prohibitions did protest, and seem to have found creative ways to do so. For instance, a large group of singers took out a mock funeral procession below the Jharokha-e-Darshan, carrying a bier, which they said bore the corpse of music. Aurangzeb's response to this kind of protest was to try and insulate himself from it; he discontinued the practice of jharokha darshan altogether, claiming that it was irreligious.[62]

In the same year, a greater austerity and orthodoxy was introduced by the emperor in court ritual. The practice of weighing the emperor against precious metals on his birthday was discontinued, and so was music at court. The stone elephants flanking the Akbarabadi Gate of the palace were removed, presumably because statues were suggestive of idols. Soon after, it was ordered that fabrics woven with gold and silver threads were not permitted by Islamic law and, therefore, were no longer to be worn be courtiers, or made a part of ceremonial robes—khilat. In 1675, the preparation of annual almanacs by the royal astrologers was prohibited. In 1677, the celebrations that used to take place on the anniversary of the emperor's coronation were also discontinued.[63]

Around the same time, Aurangzeb made drastic cuts in the imperial patronage of painting, particularly portraiture. Not all the arts were discouraged, however. Calligraphy was something that the Mughal emperors cherished and practiced themselves, and Aurangzeb was no exception. He wrote excellently in both the nastaliq and naskh variants of the Perso-Arabic scripts, mostly writing Quranic templates.[64] Ten years into his reign, Aurangzeb discontinued the practice of history writing at court, but not all kinds of writing were abandoned. His eldest daughter, Zeb-un-Nissa, was a well-educated woman. She was adept in Arabic and Persian, and wrote both prose and poetry. Moreover, she had a good collection of books, and employed and patronized many writers, poets, calligraphists and learned men.[65]

The emperor's relationship with his subjects in the capital continued to deteriorate as his reign progressed. His unpopularity in Delhi was evident in certain incidents that took place in the following years. In 1673, when he was returning after Eid celebrations, a man flung a stick at his sedan chair. The stick bounced off the corner of the sedan chair and fell on Aurangzeb's knee. However the man, whose sanity was in doubt, was released without punishment. Similar incidents happened with increasing frequency. In October 1676, when Aurangzeb was returning from the Jama Masjid, a man threw two bricks at him, one of which hit his sedan chair. The man was a follower of the Sikh Guru Tegh Bahadur. The latter had been executed almost a year before, at the kotwali. Though Aurangzeb had not been in the city at the time, the act was believed to have been carried out on his orders. It was a political execution, as the Sikhs, particularly Guru Tegh Bahadur and his followers, were at the time rising up to challenge Mughal authority.[66] Around the same time, two other attacks were made on the emperor. Once, when he was mounting his horse in front of the Diwan-e-Khas-o-Aam, a complainant threw a stick at him, which missed. On another occasion a man rushed at him with a raised sword as he was mounting his horse to return from the Jama Masjid. All these men were arrested. The emperor was also subjected to insolence—one day a water carrier casually cried out a greeting to him on the steps of the Jama Masjid.[67]

In 1679, Aurangzeb imposed a poll tax, called jizya, on Hindus throughout the empire. This was an old tax, sanctioned by the sharia, or Islamic law, but one that had been discontinued by Akbar, who wanted the Mughal state to be above sectarian differences. Aurangzeb was in his personal beliefs an orthodox Muslim, who had brought about several moral reforms ostensibly to enforce religious law. However, he did not initially set out to discriminate against his Hindu subjects. He continued the earlier Mughal policy of accommodating important Hindu elements such as the Rajputs and Marathas within the state's apparatus. The Hindu element within the mansabdars or higher bureaucracy was never higher than during his reign. However, by the late 1670s his hopes of coming to a political settlement with the Marathas had faded and the alliances between the Marathas and the kingdoms of Bijapur and Golconda were proving a threat to Mughal control in the Deccan. Aurangzeb's aggressive Muslim stance was therefore probably designed to rally the Muslim rulers of Bijapur and Golconda behind the Mughal cause, and drive a wedge between them and the Marathas—a ploy that, in fact, failed. Historians have also pointed to the dwindling revenues of the state relative to expenditure, and the unemployment among Muslim clerical elements, as motivating factors. The jizya amounted to around fifteen percent of the revenues. Moreover, this was administered by the clerical / theologian class and was spent on charity to benefit broadly the same class.[68]

The Hindus of Delhi reacted to the imposition of jizya by gathering under the Jharokha, but failing to get a response there, waylaid the emperor on his way to the Jama Masjid on Friday. According to the historian Khafi Khan, 'Money-changers and drapers, all kinds of shopkeepers from the Urdu bazaar, mechanics, and workmen of all kinds, left off work and business, and pressed into the way…it was impossible for the emperor to reach the mosque'. Ultimately the crowd was cruelly dispersed by having elephants directed against them, which led to deaths and injuries. After some days the protest died down and the Hindus of the city reconciled themselves to paying the tax.[69]

The cultural life of the city was only influenced to a limited extent by the personal inclinations of the emperor, particularly as in 1679 Aurangzeb left the city, never to return. He spent the rest of his reign occupied with campaigns in the Deccan. In the capital, painting and poetry continued to be patronized

A European depiction of the princess Jahanara.
Published in the Netherlands, around 1700.

by the nobility and members of the royal family. The former included the governor of Delhi province, Aqil Khan, who was also a poet and wrote under the pen name 'Razi'. An important royal patron was the princess Zeb-un-Nissa, at least until 1681, when she was imprisoned in Salimgarh for allegedly supporting the rebellion of Aurangzeb's son, Akbar. Jahanara, too, had returned to the capital after the death of her father in Agra in 1666. Aurangzeb treated her generously, increasing her pension from 700,000 to 12,00,000 rupees annually, out of which she was able to support a number of talented and learned individuals until her death in 1681.[70]

The support of these and other rich patrons attracted talent to the city. The prominent Persian poet of the time, Abdul Qadir 'Bedil' lived in Delhi for thirty-six years till his death in 1720. Another important poet of the late seventeenth and early eighteenth centuries was Mir Jafar 'Zatalli', known for his satirical comment on the times. He was also a pioneer of literary writing in Urdu, though it was not yet known by this name, but as Rekhta, a word that literally means 'mixed'. This was a language that was based on the Khari Boli dialect spoken in the Delhi region, enriched by many words from Persian, Turki, Punjabi and the scores of other languages spoken by the ethnically diverse population of the capital city.

The climate of religious liberalism that Delhi had enjoyed during the time of Dara Shukoh was only slightly dented by Aurangzeb's orthodoxy. Delhi had historically been a strong Sufi centre, and this continued. In fact there was a revival of the liberal Chishti silsilah of Sufis by Shaikh Kalimullah. The growth of the Chishti silsilah was also encouraged by the devotion of Jahanara.[71]

Delhi was to remain a capital without a ruler for more than thirty years. Bahadur Shah succeeded as the emperor on the death of his father, Aurangzeb, in 1707, but never entered Delhi as emperor, spending his reign fighting wars in the provinces. On his death however, his body was brought for burial near the shrine of the Sufi saint Qutubuddin Bakhtiyar Kaki. The inevitable struggle for succession among his sons ended in victory for Jahandar Shah, who rode into Delhi in June 1712. Once again the city was the capital of the empire in more than name, but a new era in both politics and culture was about to begin.

Buying arms in Delhi. Drawn by Alexis Soltykoff, 1840s.

Time of Troubles

JAHANDAR SHAH LIVED IN DELHI FROM JUNE TO DECEMBER 1712, and the whole period of his stay was an extended celebration. The emperor was highly influenced by his favourite concubine, Lal Kunwar, whom he had showered with titles and wealth, and she enjoyed great power. She was from a family of professional singers and dancers. Under the example set by her and her relatives, the imperial court adopted a culture of extreme frivolity, extravagance, drunkenness and debauchery. This considerably lowered the dignity of the imperial majesty. It was said that the contents of the treasury, which were already depleted from the wars of Aurangzeb's and Bahadur Shah's reigns, were now spent in oil for illuminating the fort and the riverbank, among other frivolities. One of the emperor's special pleasures lay in personally setting fire to the symbolic recreation of Lanka during the Dussehra festival, and enjoying fireworks on that occasion. In the meanwhile, affairs of state were allowed to slide, and soon the emperor completely lost the respect of the people of the city as well as the nobles of his empire. His aunt, Zinat-un-Nissa, the daughter of Aurangzeb, refused to see Lal Kunwar, and was therefore snubbed by the emperor.[72]

The directionless reign of Jahandar Shah was destined to be brief. A rival had arisen, in the shape of his nephew Farrukh Siyar, who crowned himself emperor mainly with the support of the Sayyid brothers—Abdullah Khan and Hussain Ali Khan. Jahandar Shah not only failed militarily against the rival forces, he had also lost the support of the people of the city. Even before Farrukh Siyar arrived in the city, his name was included as emperor in the khutba or sermon read at the Jama Masjid. Jahandar Shah was executed on 11 February 1713, and the next day Farrukh Siyar ceremoniously entered the city. The new emperor rode on an elephant, and behind him on another elephant sat an executioner holding aloft the head of Jahandar Shah impaled on a pole. His body followed, slung over the back of a third elephant. The body then lay for a few days in the sands outside the Delhi Gate of the city, before being buried in Humayun's tomb.[73]

If Jahandar Shah's rule had been characterized by frivolity and mismanagement, Farrukh Siyar's opened with a reign of terror. The emperor was unable to keep different powerful nobles and factions at his court in check, and, as a result, the various rivalries were played out in a bloody manner. During previous contests for the throne, the victor had invariably pardoned nobles from his defeated rival's camp and incorporated them into his court. Now, on the other hand, there was a spate of assassinations and executions, often at the behest of various nobles of the victorious camp.[74]

The violence of Farrukh Siyar's reign was commemorated by the satirist Jafar Zatalli, thus:

> He struck his coins on grains of wheat
> And on coarse pulses, and peas;
> Farrukh Siyar, the garrotter of a king.[75]

Zatalli was executed for his impertinence.

There were however some moments of lightness and celebration too, such as the December 1715 wedding of Farrukh Siyar with the Princess of Jodhpur, Bai Indar Kunwar. The sight of the emperor emerging from the Delhi Gate of the palace, dressed in his wedding clothes and seated on a movable throne, provided a spectacle for the people of the city. A matter that caused some talk was that the bride's party, who were Rajputs, prepared a drink according to their custom, which was made of rosewater, sugar and opium. Many of the groom's party drank it. Some however objected on the grounds that intoxicants were not acceptable to them on religious grounds.[76]

A far more sombre spectacle occurred in March 1716, with the arrival of hundreds of Sikh prisoners, together with their leader, Banda Singh Bahadur. Though Bahadur Shah had been on amicable terms with Guru Govind Singh, after his death in 1708, Banda Bahadur had assumed leadership of the Sikhs and adopted a much more aggressive stance towards the Mughal empire. During Farrukh Siyar's reign, Banda Bahadur's forces were defeated after a prolonged siege at Gurdaspur. The prisoners were subsequently paraded through the streets of Delhi and publicly put to death. Even for the people of Delhi, inured as they were by now to such bloody scenes, this was a horrific spectacle, as for a whole week, each day a hundred prisoners were publicly executed at the kotwali chabutra—the public platform in front of the kotwali. The Khatri traders of the city, who were followers of Banda, put together a large sum of money as a ransom for the leader, but could not secure his release.[77]

As Farukh Siyar's rule progressed, there was increasing mismanagement, born of the emperor's incompetence and the deadly rivalries between important nobles. The contest for control over the emperor broke into open armed conflict on 28 February 1719. On one side were the Sayyids and on the other were most of the nobles, including the Rajput chiefs. The Sayyids had brought to the conflict some eleven thousand Maratha troops too, but 1,500-2,000 of these were killed in the streets of the city. The main battle happened just outside the two main gates of the fort—from where the Sayyids' artillery fired on their enemies surrounding the fort. The Sayyid brothers were victorious before the day ended. The damage to the city mainly consisted of the plundered houses in the neighbourhood of the Delhi Gate.[78]

The emperor was dragged out of the private apartments where he was hiding, blinded and imprisoned, and finally executed two months later. A huge crowd, some 15,000 to 20,000, joined his funeral procession, and many others watched from roofs and doors as it passed. Evidently, the people of Delhi had a sense of loyalty to the Mughal family, and expressed their protest when an emperor, whatever his shortcomings, was so unceremoniously dealt with. The funeral procession was greeted with vocal lamentation and tears, particularly by the common people. Contemporary observers noted that 'The rabble and the mendicants, who had received alms from Farrukh Siyar, followed his bier, rending their garments and throwing ashes on their heads, and as it passed, the women on the roofs raised their cry of mourning, and flung stones and bricks upon the servants and officers of the Sayyids'. The body was buried in Humayun's tomb, and for a while food was distributed in charity from here every Thursday. This was arranged by the beggars or mendicants, who collected money from shopkeepers and artisans of the city. Many of these people also publicly abused all of the nobles who were complicit in the fate that had befallen Farrukh Siyar.[79]

While the common people of the city expressed themselves through these means of popular protest, the educated elite used literary tools. Abdul Qadir 'Bedil', the preeminent Persian language poet of his time, wrote a scathing comment on the death of Farrukh Siyar, in the form of a chronogram. It consisted of one line that read: 'The Sayyids behaved disloyally to their king.' This was not however the only opinion held by the literati. Another poet, Mir Azmat Ullah 'Bekhabar', composed another chronogram for the same date, saying: 'The Sayyids treated him as the case required.'[80]

The Sayyid brothers placed two puppets on the throne in quick succession—Farrukh Siyar's cousin, Rafi-ud-Darajat, followed by his older brother, Rafi-ud-Daulah. Both soon died from the effects of opium addiction. The Sayyid brothers then put on the throne a seventeen-year-old grandson of Bahadur Shah, Roshan Akhtar, who ascended the throne in September 1719 with the title Muhammad Shah. But the fall of the Sayyid brothers was imminent, given the number of enemies they had. Husain Ali Khan was assassinated in a political plot in 1720, and in the same year Abdullah Khan was defeated in battle.[81]

Upheaval of a different kind occurred in Delhi in the same year. On 27 June, there was a strong earthquake, which destroyed or damaged many buildings, and killed around a dozen people. Many aftershocks were felt over the next four to five months.[82]

Having shaken off the influence of the Sayyid brothers, Muhammad Shah came into his own as a ruler. One of the first measures he adopted was the abolition of the jizya.[83] However, it was soon apparent that the emperor was not particularly capable. He paid little attention to affairs of state, which were left in the hands of incompetent and venal people who from time to time became favourites of the emperor and his powerful mother, Qudsiya Begum. They ran an unpopular, corrupt and inefficient administration, though Qudsiya Begum was described by one historian as being 'a woman of much intelligence and tact'.[84]

The inefficient administration of the city led in 1729 to what is known as the shoe-sellers' riot. This began as an altercation between a jeweller of the imperial karkhana or workshop, called Shubh Karan, and some Punjabi shoe-sellers. The issue was a petty one—the shoe-sellers were letting off some fireworks on the street, and a spark landed on Shubh Karan's palanquin as he was going home. This led to violence between the two sides, and ultimately to the shoe-sellers gathering together a mob, which stormed the Jama Masjid, obstructing worship and calling for justice.[85]

The empire was also starting to break up. One of the highest nobles of the empire, Nizam-ul-Mulk, who had been appointed prime minister of the empire early in the reign of Mohammad Shah, resigned in 1724. From then on he spent most of his time in the southern province of the Deccan, of which he was the governor. Here he founded what was practically an independent state, that of Hyderabad. Sa'adat Khan, the governor of Awadh, similarly established his independence and a dynastic succession in that province. The province of Bengal, Bihar and Orissa had also become virtually independent under its successive Mughal subedars.

The Marathas, meanwhile, had become a formidable regional power in Western India, and in 1737, under the command of Baji Rao, arrived at the very threshold of Delhi.

The first sign of their unexpected appearance was an attack on people gathered for a Ram Navami fair, which was being held at the Kalka Devi temple, some twelve to thirteen kilometres to the south of the city. After this the attackers camped at Malcha, to the south-west of the city. At the time most of the imperial forces were out of the capital, leaving it largely undefended. A very inexperienced and inadequate force was sent out to confront the Marathas, who comprehensively trounced the imperial army, leaving some 600 dead. The swift retreat into the city of the routed troops, carrying their wounded and dead, caused a panic. The Marathas, however, had learnt of the approach of the main imperial army, which was heading towards the capital, and therefore vanished from Delhi as quickly as they had come.[86]

An even more calamitous event was the invasion of Nadir Shah, the ethnic Turk ruler of Iran. Nadir Shah crossed the empire's north-west frontier, in Afghanistan, in May 1738. He followed this with a leisurely but inexorable march towards Delhi, on the way conquering Mughal forts and towns in the provinces of Afghanistan and Punjab. The disorganization in the Mughal empire was such that he only met very half-hearted resistance. In the battle that took place in February 1739 at Karnal, Nadir Shah's army decisively defeated the Mughal force.[87] A humiliating peace was then made, contingent on a huge indemnity, with which the invading army would return. Before this, an elaborate display was to take place in the Mughal capital, so that Nadir Shah could formally proclaim his victory. Muhammad Shah entered the city first, on 8

March. The procession was a sombre one, with no ceremonial music or banners accompanying the emperor, who rode on a portable throne on the back of an elephant. Nadir Shah rode in on a horse the next day, from Shalimar Bagh, where he had been camping. His mounted troops lined the road from the garden to the city. He entered the palace complex and was ceremonially and lavishly received by Muhammad Shah, who vacated his own palace for him.[88]

On 10 March was the festival of Eid-ul-Zuha, and on that day the name of Nadir Shah was proclaimed as sovereign in the sermon or khutba of the mosques of the city. Coins were also struck in his name, and remained current for two months. Within the fort, Nadir Shah made a show of graciously allowing Muhammad Shah to retain his throne, and the latter laid out a vast treasure as an offering. This was in effect the ransom demanded by the conqueror. As Muhammad Mehdi, the chronicler of Nadir Shah remarked, this consisted of 'the accumulated treasure stores and rare possessions of the rulers of Dilli…the piled-up wealth of all the other kings of the world did not amount to a tenth part of a tenth part of this immense treasure'.[89]

While the emperor quietly acquiesced to the demands of the Iranian ruler within the palace, in the city outside, trouble was brewing. Shahjahanabad had always had a section of the population that was by nature turbulent, easily inflamed and prone to mob violence. The seed of the present trouble was sown by a rumour that Nadir Shah had been killed within the palace. This news incited the rabble to immediately attack the stray soldiers of Nadir Shah's army, who had entered the city and were casually wandering about. According to some observers, the fact that it was the eve of the festival of Holi, was also a factor, as many of the attackers were intoxicated. The soldiers were caught off guard and were at a disadvantage in a city whose language and narrow lanes they were unfamiliar with. The belief that their emperor was dead no doubt had a disheartening effect too. As a consequence some 3,000 of the Irani soldiers were killed.[90]

The violence had been unplanned, and was perpetrated by an anonymous mob. It was also very unwise, given that the bulk of the conquering army was stationed just outside the city walls. The next morning, a terrible vengeance was extracted by Nadir Shah for this affront. The neighbourhoods where the violence had occurred were identified, and in these, a massacre was ordered. From nine o'clock in the morning till two in the afternoon, the Iranian soldiers killed men and captured women for slaves. Shops and homes were looted and burnt. Nadir Shah himself sat on the terrace of the mosque of Roshan-ud-Daula (called the Sunehri Masjid), at the Kotwali Chowk, and superintended the punishment. He finally commanded his soldiers to stop only when Muhammad Shah sent his highest nobles to beg his forgiveness. Widely varying estimates of the number killed were given by various observers, but they probably amounted to some twenty thousand. A few days later the kotwal collected the bodies of victims on roads and in open spaces, where they were burnt.[91]

Nadir Shah stayed in Delhi for the next two months,

during which a huge indemnity was extracted from the city. This was paid not only by the emperor, the nobles, and the rich merchants, but by each citizen according to his means. A sum of twenty million rupees was extracted from the citizens of Delhi, apart from what was paid by the nobles and the emperor. The emperor gave up magnificent jewels, including the Kohinoor diamond, and the famous jewelled Peacock Throne that had been commissioned by Shahjahan. His ministers surrendered their own vast treasures too. In all, Nadir Shah took back with him more than half a billion rupees worth of treasure. This enabled him to forego the collection of revenue within his own kingdom for the next three years, and to reward his soldiers richly.[92]

The resilient population of the capital city soon recovered from this too. In fact, throughout this period, though the empire and court lurched from one crisis to another, and the city faced calamities of loot and massacre, a lively social scene remained remarkably intact. The capacity of the citizens of Shahjahanabad to enjoy themselves was particularly noticed by visitors. One of these was Dargah Quli Khan, a nobleman who had come from the Deccan in the entourage of Nizam-ul-Mulk, and lived in Delhi for about three years, from 1738 to 1741. Though this was the period during which the disastrous attack of Nadir Shah took place, Dargah Quli's account focuses almost exclusively on the hedonistic lifestyle of the residents of the city.[93]

The example set by the court and the patronage of the nobility played a great part in the importance of courtesans,

A depiction of a dance performance, drawn by John Luard and published in 1838.

both male and female, in the society of the time. Dargah Quli describes some of the courtesans, and was very taken by their beauty and elegant bearing. They were beautiful, good conversationalists and talented in singing and dancing. Some of them were exclusively connected to rich patrons, but others seem to have been quite independent, and we are told that their company could only be secured through rich presents and the right recommendations.[94] A famous courtesan of the time was Nur Bai, who enjoyed a rich lifestyle. She had a large and beautiful house and when she went out, she rode on an elephant with accompanying heralds and mace-bearers. Apart from being an accomplished singer, she had a critical taste in poetry, brilliant conversational skills and an extremely sophisticated manner. Not surprisingly, her company came at a high price. It was rumoured that many had squandered their fortunes for the pleasure of her company.[95] Those less talented could rely on sensationalism. One courtesan was notorious for her style of dress, for instead of wearing any garment on her lower limbs, she would have her skin painted to mimic fabric. This would then show through her sheer outer clothing, and until closely scrutinized, would give the appearance of a garment.[96]

A variety of talents were given patronage by the royal court and the rich of the city. Muhammad Shah patronized more than one troupe of entertainers, who had acts that included singing, magical tricks and mimicry, and dance performances by young men. His wazir, Qamar-ud-din Khan, was himself one of the biggest patrons of gatherings where wine and other intoxicants flowed, and people were entertained by performers. Since the well-to-do aspired to copy the example set by the court, several similar entertainers, specializing in play-acting, comedy and mimicry, could make a living from their art.[97]

In his account Dargah Quli mentions meeting a large number of musicians. Among singers he includes the descendants of Tansen (the great sixteenth-century musician who was a contemporary of Akbar), and several singers of qawwali. He also met players of various musical instruments such as the been (a wind instrument), the tambur, rabab, sarangi (string instruments), and the pakhawaj, dholak, dhamdhami, (percussion instruments). Many of these were patronized by the court and the nobility, and we hear of musical sessions and gatherings being organized in the homes of patrons. Some of the singers were so much sought after, that their patrons put up with their idiosyncrasies, such as drunkenness. Several regular gatherings were also organized in the homes of the singers themselves.[98]

Appreciation of poetry was an important part of the cultural climate of eighteenth-century Shahjahanabad. Urdu as a literary language had come into its own, but Persian poetry too continued to be composed, though it had a more elite following. Gatherings of poets, or mushairas, took place in the homes of high nobles who were often poets themselves, but also in more modest homes. A gathering of poets was also held annually at the grave of the poet Abdul Qadir 'Bedil' (who had died in 1720), outside the wall of the city, to the south. Poets used to gather here on the anniversary of Bedil's death, place the poet's collected works in their midst, and recite his and their own poetry.[99]

The eighteenth century was the era of the great masters of poetry—Mir Taqi 'Mir', Mirza Mohammad Rafi 'Sauda', Khwaja Mir 'Dard' and several others. Around these masters, or ustads, gathered a large number of disciples, or shagirds, who received instruction in the fairly complex conventions and rules which governed classical poetry.[100] The testing ground for this poetry was the mushaira. Various poets would be invited to recite their verse at these gatherings, which were organized in the Mughal court or in the homes of rich patrons. At the mushaira, the conventional order of precedence dictated that acknowledged masters would recite last. This caused occasional clashes of ego, as it became an important matter of prestige for the poets concerned. The mushaira was particularly important because it was the forum where a poet's work was tested, and he faced the opinion of his peers. It was where practically every new verse was first aired. How an individual's poetry was received and whether verses recited by him were on people's lips the next morning, was crucial in determining his success and reputation. Mushairas sometimes became the venue for sparring between two ustads, who usually involved their respective shagirds in the battle. Verses would fly back and forth as they tried to outdo each other in difficulty and originality, while being careful not to overstep the bounds of language and imagery prescribed by the conventions of Urdu and Persian poetics.[101]

Entertainment and the arts were not a preserve only of

exclusive gatherings. As in the previous century, one important public place known for its entertainers was Chowk Sa'adullah Khan. As before, this square, close to the southern entrance to the Red Fort, was where public dance performances took place, but now not only by women, but also young men. There were also young male singers who were immensely popular and earned so much money here that they turned down invitations to perform at private homes. Qissa go—professional storytellers—plied their trade, attracting listeners with their fascinating tales, told in a beguiling style. Among the other entertainers were mimics. Preachers too installed themselves atop wooden stools and delivered sermons suited to the religious calendar. For instance, during the month of Muharram, they recited the tragedy of Karbala in such an evocative style that the listening crowds were moved to tears, and happily contributed offerings of coins. Astrologers, diviners, quacks making fabulous claims for their medicines, particularly aphrodisiacs, all attracted large numbers of credulous customers. A wide variety of goods too was sold in the chowk—weapons, fabrics, fruits, wild animals, particularly birds.[102]

Chandni Chowk, the market established by Jahanara Begum, had shops dealing in commodities of all sorts—fabrics, weapons, china, glassware. This square was where the rich and noble, as well as more humble citizens, came to spend time and shop. Chandni Chowk was also known for its kahwe khane, or coffee shops, which were popular meeting places. Poets frequently met here informally and recited their newest poetry and received the criticism of their peers.[103]

It was not just the pleasures of the flesh that preoccupied the people of Shahjahanabad in this era. While many escaped the uncertainties and tribulations of the troubled times in pursuit of worldly desires, an equal number found solace in spiritual and religious pursuits, and in fact many did both. Interest in religion is evidenced by the number of temples and mosques that were built during this time. Two important Jain temples, the Vaidwara temple, and the Panchayati Mandir, near Masjid Khajur, were built in 1741 and 1743, soon after the sack of the city by Nadir Shah. This shows that the rich Jain merchants had not been completely ruined. In fact, it is probable that the impoverished emperor's reliance on these rich merchants increased, for Jain histories say that, for a while at least, an imperial ban on animal slaughter had been imposed at the request of the rich Jains.[104]

Spiritual men of all shades of belief and practice, also had large followings. The rich flocked to them for spiritual guidance and solace, and made offerings, which in turn were used to feed the many poor who came to the pirs not only for spiritual, but temporal succour.[105] The shrines and seats of some Sufi saints were also important centres for music, particularly the qawwali genre. Qawwali was devotional singing closely connected to the Sufi tradition, and in particular, the dargahs or shrines of the Chishti silsilah or order.[106] Some of the prominent Sufis of the period were also well-known poets, such as Mirza Mazhar Jan-e-Janan and Mir Dard.

The world of the Sufi shrines and the pleasure palaces of the city were not far removed from each other, as is evident in Dargah Quli's description of the festival of Basant, or spring, held every year. The festival was celebrated over several days, in turn, at different shrines in and around the city—Qadam Sharif, Qutubuddin Bakhtiyar Kaki, Nasiruddin Chiragh-e-Dehli, Nizamuddin Auliya, Hasan Rasul Numa, Shah Turkman. The picture that is painted is as much one of sensory experiences as devotion. Lavish floral decorations, the showering of elaborate perfumes on the devotees, devotional singing with musical accompaniment, imbued the spiritual experience with a strong sensory component. On the seventh night of the festival, the gathering moved to a more obscure grave, which was then washed with wine, and here the festival concluded with a night of dancing and intoxication.[107]

To some, these unorthodox practices represented a deplorable moral laxity, which afflicted both state and society. One such observer was Shah Waliullah, the most prominent Islamic teacher and reformer of the eighteenth century. Shah Waliullah attempted to use his influence to correct both state and society. Through a series of letters, he tried to give guidance to important members of the imperial government, to run the administration in an efficient and honest manner. His attempts to reform society mainly lay in his seeking to correct the practices of his fellow-Muslims. He felt that an important step toward this was for them to understand the tenets of their religion well. He translated the Quran from Arabic to Persian (the latter being a language that most educated Muslims understood), with the aim of making it understood to a larger number of people. He also propagated his ideas on religious and social reform through a large number of books and pamphlets, and an important educational institution, or madrasa, run by him.[108]

Muhammad Shah, weakened by a dissipated lifestyle, which included an addiction to opium, died in 1748. He was succeeded by his 22-year-old son Ahmad Shah, who had neither the ability nor the inclination to be an able ruler. Affairs of state were left in the hands of his mother, also titled Qudsiya Begum, like her mother-in-law, and Javed Khan.

Qudsiya Begum had been a dancing girl called Udham Bai before she married Muhammad Shah. She came into her own with the accession of her son, receiving high titles, honours and sources of revenue. Qudsiya Begum was responsible for laying out a garden just outside the Kashmiri Gate of the city, which still goes by her name. She also commissioned a small mosque just south of the Red Fort, which came to be called Sunehri Masjid.

Qudsiya Begum took a close interest in all affairs of state and, seated behind a screen, would consult with the high officials of state and pass orders. Her ally was Javed Khan, who had been the chief eunuch of the harem during the reign of Muhammad Shah. Though he was illiterate, he soon gained great influence and control through the trust that the Begum placed in him.[109]

Their power did not last long. A powerful force within the nobility was Safdar Jang, who had succeeded his father-in-law Sa'adat Khan as the governor of Awadh and had become the wazir of the empire in 1748. Safdar Jang managed to gain

Qudsiya Bagh, painted by Thomas and Willliam Daniell. Published in 1795.

the upper hand for a while by having Javed Khan murdered in 1752, but he had other enemies at court. He was forced to leave for Awadh the following year, but not before a prolonged civil war in which the city, particularly the area outside the walls, was devastated.[110]

Prolonged warfare destroyed the finances of the court. The armies could not be paid, and as a result they rioted in the streets and burnt and looted the shops and homes of the better-off. Jat and Maratha troops, used by the powerful Mughal nobles as their allies in their personal battles, gathered outside the city walls, destroying villages and suburbs and plundering the population. Refugees poured into the city. The emperor made arrangements for them to be accommodated in the various imperial buildings that were vacated for the purpose, and in imperial gardens including Bagh Sahibabad, where they were provided relief.[111]

After the departure of Safadar Jang, Imad-ul-Mulk, the grandson of Nizam-ul-Mulk, was the new power at Delhi. He proved to be every bit as malevolent a force as Safdar Jang had been. Ahmad Shah was deposed and imprisoned in 1754. His successor Alamgir II, was murdered in 1759. The latter's eldest son, Ali Gauhar (later Shah Alam II), just about escaped with his life, fleeing to Awadh. Now another prince was put on the throne with the title Shahjahan II.[112]

In the meanwhile, there was yet another invader at the city's gates. Ahmad Shah Abdali, who had succeeded to the Afghan provinces of Nadir Shah on the latter's assassination in 1747, soon after made deep inroads into the Punjab province of the Mughal empire. In 1757, he arrived in Delhi and the court and city went through the same routine of surrender and supplication as they had with Nadir Shah. Extreme violence was used in the extraction of loot, and a large treasure was taken back by the invader. Among the prizes were several princesses from the royal family. Remarkably, the emperor's parting request of Abdali was for the release of the several thousand poor men and women who were being taken away as slaves, and this was granted.[113]

Imad-ul-Mulk's attempts to consolidate his position with the help of the Marathas was thwarted by his rival at court, Najib Khan Ruhela, who was supported by Ahmad Shah Abdali. The Marathas and the supporters of Abdali warred repeatedly from 1760—for control over the imperial city, which passed from one to the other conqueror. The loot of the city and the palace complex continued. In 1760 the Marathas stripped the silver from the ceiling of the Diwan-e-Khas and minted it into coins worth 900,000 rupees. The Maratha commander, Sadashiv Bhau, bathed at Nigambodh Ghat on the no-moon day in the month of Sawan (August), and distributed alms amongst Brahmins and Muslim mendicants.[114]

The defeat of the Marathas by Ahmad Shah Abdali, at the battle of Panipat in January 1761, put Delhi under the control of Najib Khan, and after him, his son, Zabita Khan. Ali Gauhar had succeeded to the throne in 1760 as Shah Alam II, but remained in exile in Awadh. Though his mother and his heir, Jawan Bakht, were in the city, he feared to return to it, because Shahjahanabad's troubles were far from over. Najib Khan just about held the city, fending off attacks and sieges by the Jats, Marathas and Sikhs, which left the city reeling under bombardments from the besieging armies and pressed by food shortages.[115]

Ten years after the debacle at Panipat, the Marathas had recovered sufficiently to once more play a determining role in North Indian politics. Shah Alam II negotiated with them a return to his capital under their protection. On 6 January 1772, he entered the city and his palace, on the eve of the Eid-ul-Fitr celebrations.[116] The return of the emperor did not change very much in the city. The tussles between the various nobles at court continued, and the city was battered by civil war as well as by raids by the Sikhs and Gujjars. In addition to the hardships of war and disorder, by the end of the decade Delhi was also hit by natural calamities—famine due to drought in 1780, and a severe earthquake in 1781.[117]

Finally, in 1784, the emperor effectively gave over the reins of the empire to the Marathas. The latter were at that moment a strong force in North India, and Shah Alam II hoped that the chieftain, Mahadji Sindhia, would be able to restore some order in the few remaining territories of the empire and extract enough revenue to meet the dire needs of the empire and the royal household. The Peshwa, who was the titular head of the Marathas, was formally appointed the regent of the empire, as well as commander-in-chief, on the condition that his functions were to be executed by Mahadji Sindhia.[118]

Sindhia however soon learned that his task was not an easy one, and found himself engaged in prolonged warfare with the many recalcitrant forces in North India—particularly the state of Jaipur—and he suffered several military setbacks. Mahadji Sindhia's preoccupations elsewhere resulted in certain developments in Delhi that have gone down in the history of the Mughal dynasty for their bloodiness. Ghulam Qadir, the son of Zabita Khan and grandson of Najib Khan, hoped to gain by force of arms the high positions that his father and grandfather had enjoyed. He captured Delhi in 1787, and forced the emperor to grant him high office and the jagirs that went with it. Perhaps the only resistance he encountered in Delhi was from the forces of Begum Samru, whose troops protected the emperor. Named Farzana, Begum Samru was a Kashmiri dancing girl who had married the European military freelancer Walter Reinhardt 'Sombre'. Sombre had come to India in the middle of the eighteenth century and made his fortune as a military soldier. His nickname, Sombre, was corrupted to Samru, and his widow is best known by this name. After his death, the Begum inherited his estate of Sardhana, and also successfully commanded his military force, which was led by efficient French mercenary soldiers.[119]

Ghulam Qadir overcame the opposition, particularly as he had the support of traitors within Delhi. These included the chief eunuch of the harem, Nazir Manzur Ali, who wanted to use this new power to counter the Marathas; and certain members of the royal family who held grudges against the emperor. Among the latter was Mallika-e-Zamani, the widow of Mohammad Shah, whose stepson, the emperor Ahmad Shah, had been blinded and deposed by Shah Alam II's father. She gave Ghulam Qadir a sum of twelve hundred thousand rupees to replace Shah Alam II with Bedar Bakht, the son of Ahmad Shah. Efforts made by the emperor to oust Ghulam Qadir enraged the latter, and he exacted a heavy vengeance on the royal family. Shah Alam was blinded, and members of the royal family as well as other members of the royal household, were insulted, tortured and starved, and the treasures in the palace looted. Mallika-e-Zamani and Nazir Manzur Ali were not spared either.[120]

Ghulam Qadir's terror over the palace and the city lasted for a period of over two months, till the Marathas arrived in October 1788, and managed to drive him out. Ghulam Qadir was hunted down by Mahadji Sindhia, and when caught, his eyeballs, nose and ears were severed from his head and sent to Delhi in a casket to satisfy the emperor. The Sindhia chiefs—Mahadji Sindhia and after him, his successor Daulat Rao, however, were soon preoccupied again with trouble in their dominions, including tussles with other Maratha sardars. Delhi continued to be mismanaged by the administrators and military commanders that were put in charge.[121]

The political uncertainty and military conflict that afflicted the city through most of the eighteenth century took a heavy toll in terms of social and economic life. The poets of the city commented on the sufferings of the people. Sauda, the greatest satirist of the age wrote:

> *Kharab hain woh imarat kya kahun tujh paas*
> *ke jis ke dekhe se jati thi bhookh o pyaas*
> *aur ab jo dekhe to dil howe zindagi se udaas*
> *bajaye gul chamanon mein, kamar kamar hai ghas*
> *kahin sutun pada hai, kahin pade marghol.*[122]

> The lovely buildings which once made the famished man forget his hunger, are in ruins now.
> In the once-beautiful gardens, where the nightingale sang his love songs to the rose, the grass grows waist-high around the fallen pillars and ruined arches.[123]

Sauda migrated from the city in 1757, like many other men of talent who were forced to seek elsewhere for their livelihood. His contemporary, Mir, was one of the last to leave. He stayed till 1782, when he too was forced to migrate. He went to live in Lucknow, where there were still patrons who could enable a poet to earn his living. Mir memorialized the city he had left behind in these poignant words:

> *Kya bood o baash poochho ho purab ke sakinon*
> *ham ko gharib jaan ke, hansi hansi pukar ke*
> *dilli jo ek shahar tha aalam mein intikhab*
> *rahte the muntakhab hi jahan rozgar ke*
> *usko falak ne loot ke viraan kar diya*
> *hum rahne wale hain usi ujde dayar ke.*

Why do you mock at me and ask yourselves
Where in the world I come from, easterners?
There was a city, famed throughout the world,
Where dwelt the chosen spirits of the age:
Delhi its name, fairest among the fair.
Fate looted it and laid it desolate,
And to that ravaged city I belong.[124]

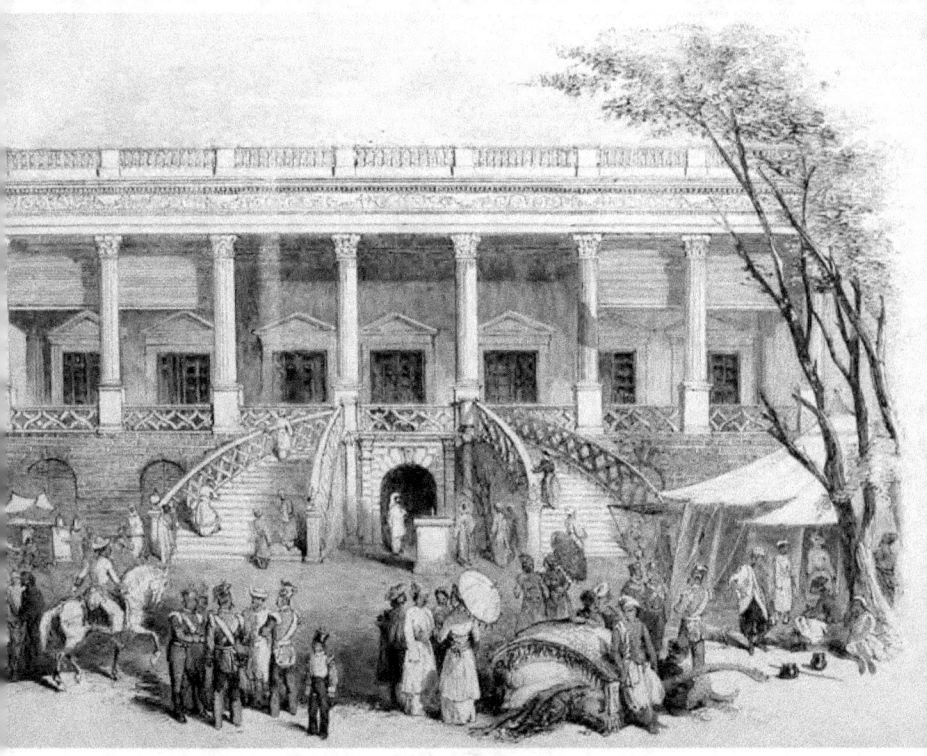

Begum Samru's House, in a newspaper illustration from 1857.

The East India Company's Administration

NEARLY A CENTURY OF POLITICAL UPHEAVAL CAME TO AN END in September 1803, when the Maratha forces were defeated by the army of the British East India Company, under the command of General Lake, at the battle of Patparganj, across the river from the capital. The British had been steadily gaining ground, advancing from their base in Bengal, till, in the early nineteenth century, they established their dominance in North India too.

The British took over Delhi after their victory, and Shah Alam II made the transition from being the puppet of the Marathas to that of the East India Company.[125] The relationship of the emperor with the new power was similar to what it had been with the Marathas. In formal terms, the Company was the 'protector' of the emperor and the principal functionary of the empire on his behalf. From now on, the administration of the city was in the hands of the East India Company's officials. Though the nomenclature varied from time to time, the highest officials were the Commissioner, and the Resident/Agent to the Governor General, and often these posts were combined in the person of one individual.

The emperor's jurisdiction only extended to those living within the walls of the Red Fort. These included the large extended royal family. By this time, this was quite large, including descendants of many previous emperors from their wives and concubines, and various other branches of the family. The household also included a large number of domestic and other employees, as had been the case before.

Shah Alam II died in 1806, and was succeeded by his son Akbar II. Quite early in his reign a difference of opinion arose as to who would be his successor. The Mughals had never followed primogeniture; there was no expectation that the eldest son would succeed his father. Even in the heyday of the empire, though a father often made his own preference clear, the sons would fight it out amongst themselves. This had happened during the accession of Aurangzeb and even of Shahjahan himself. Akbar II's eldest son was Abu Zafar, a scholarly, cultured and unassuming man, and the Company supported his candidature as the future emperor. But Akbar II clearly favoured a younger son, Jahangir, born to him of his favourite wife, Mumtaz Mahal. Jahangir was spoilt, wilful and unruly.

While the British government were interested in cutting Jahangir down to size, they were even more interested in gaining military control of the Red Fort, which was guarded by the emperor's troops. The Resident, Archibald Seton, bullied and persuaded the emperor into having British troops stationed at the two gates of the Fort—the Lahori and Delhi Gates. Many members of the royal family and others within the fort were opposed to this move, but Jahangir, true to character, took drastic measures. He and his armed followers took up a position in the windows and galleries of buildings commanding a view of the British post. Seton arrived on the scene and as he was advancing, with the intention, as he later described, of reasoning with the prince, he was fired upon. The bullet went harmlessly through the cap of a soldier next to him. Seton retreated and after some attempt at negotiation, British guns were turned on the gates of the fort, which were blown open. Jahangir was taken into custody and the Company's troops occupied the fort.[126]

As a punishment, Jahangir was exiled to Allahabad. His loving parents were devastated. They agreed to the investiture of Zafar as the heir apparent, in order to conciliate Seton, in the hope that Jahangir would be allowed to return. The reward was the return of Jahangir. The prince arrived back in Delhi in November 1810 after an absence of little over a year.[127] While he was away, his mother, Mumtaz Mahal, had taken a vow that she would offer a canopy and coverlet of flowers at the shrine of Qutubuddin Bakhtiyar Kaki if her son returned to Delhi. When he returned, this was done with great pomp. The flower sellers of the city, who were commissioned to prepare the floral offerings, added pankhas or fans, to the procession, on their own accord. The queen, as well as a large number of the people of the palace and the city, went in a procession to Mehrauli where the coverlet of flowers was offered at the shrine of Qutubuddin Bakhtiyar Kaki, and the fans at the temple of the goddess Yog Maya. This proved to be so popular, that this was the start of the annual festival known as the Phulwalon ki Sair—literally 'spectacle of the flower sellers'. This is a festival that has survived till present times. It had been banned during the Quit India Movement in 1942, but was again revived in the 1960s.[128]

Jahangir, however, soon went back to Allahabad; this time of his own accord. He knew he could never aspire to the throne, and if his father died while he was at Delhi, he would be under the authority of Zafar, who would be emperor. The British readily agreed to the request, happy to remove what they considered to be a disruptive influence within the palace.

Once in Allahabad, he was never allowed to return to Delhi. He died there in 1821, a premature death brought on by his addiction to alcohol.[129]

Akbar II died in 1837, and Zafar, as soon as he heard that the old king had died, insisted on ascending the throne in the middle of the night, against the advice of his astrologers. Soon after, there was a widespread famine in India, which was attributed in Delhi to the act of the new emperor. Food riots took place when grain arrived in boats in Delhi. This became a memorable landmark event in the lives of the people. A poem commemorating this event, and rather unflattering to Bahadur Shah, the title that Zafar now adopted, was composed and became popular in the city.[130]

Whatever the concerns of the royal family, the first half of the nineteenth century was a period of recovery for the people of the city. As the East India Company vanquished its enemies, the continuous warfare that had characterized North India over the previous several decades, came to a close. With peace being achieved, trade and agriculture began to recover, and consequently, so did the fortunes of the people of Delhi. Property prices rose, new houses were built, and the population, which had dipped sharply during the late eighteenth century, began to rise again. By the mid-nineteenth century the people living within the city walls numbered 1,37,977, of which there were 66,120 Muslims, 71,530 Hindus and Jains, and 327 others.[131]

Religious affiliation was an important and evolving element in the self-perception of the people of the city. Delhi was an important centre of Islamic learning as well as the seat of important Sufi saints. The sons of Shah Waliullah, the great teacher of the eighteenth century, carried on his tradition of reforming the customs and practices of Muslims into the nineteenth century. They taught numerous students, many of whom came from far away. They also gave spiritual guidance in the Sufi tradition to initiated disciples. At the same time, the brothers reached out to a broader public. One way of doing this was preaching in the mosques of Delhi, and another was through fatwas. Fatwas, opinions of experts on points of sharia law, became the source of fairly detailed guidance for individual Muslims seeking to lead a life in accordance with the shari'at, particularly in the context of alien rule.[132]

By the third decade of the nineteenth century, a radical strand in the Muslim reform movement was calling for a rejection of some popular socio-religious practices on the grounds that they were unIslamic. Among those who took this position were Mohammad Ismail and Abdul Hayy, the nephew and son-in-law of Shah Abdul Aziz. This radicalization put them on a collision course with their own co-religionists. Sufism was sought to be cleansed of popular accretions such as meditation on the image of the saint, prostration at shrines, circumambulation and sanctifying water. This and other doctrinal stands generated considerable opposition, with eminent religious scholars ranged on the other side. The doctrinal strife was expressed through pamphleteering and public disputations. Soon, potentially sensitive addresses at the Jama Masjid and other mosques had to be attended by police presence. Certain popular Shia practices, such as the making of taziyahs, were also denounced by the reformers with a vehemence that was uncharacteristic of the earlier generation of Abdul Aziz and his brothers. In fact by mid-century, Moharram had become an annual occasion for animosity between Shias and Sunnis, necessitating police arrangements and leading to occasional violent incidents.[133]

The Muslim reform movement did not lead to conflict with those of other faiths, but conflicts sometimes arose from different reasons. One underlying factor was that the position of the Muslim elite had been based mainly on landed income and positions within the Mughal bureaucracy. With the establishment of British rule, many of the old landed gentry lost their estates, and the openings in the higher administration dried up. On the other hand, many of the Hindu and Jain elite of Delhi, whose fortunes were connected with trade, prospered under the improving economic climate. They now began to assert their position, through means such as ostentatious religious celebrations and a questioning of the Muslims' right to ritual cow slaughter. The British had reversed the prohibition on cow slaughter, which had existed in Delhi immediately before their advent. Now, Muslims were allowed to sacrifice the animals within their own houses on Eid-ul-Zuha, away from the houses of Hindus. By the 1850s, the issue became a festering problem leading to much bitterness, year after year. The Hindus and Jains would lay petitions before the administration calling for an absolute ban. The Muslims would, in turn, make it a point to carry out sacrifices in areas considered impermissible by the Hindus, who would then retaliate with measures such as defiling mosques.[134]

On the whole, however, apart from these occasional outbreaks, sectarian strife was uncommon. People lived together quite amicably, participating in each other's festivals and celebrations. For instance, Holi was celebrated by Muslims as well as Hindus.[135] In this regard, in fact, a leading role was played by the Mughal royal family. Several Hindu festivals were celebrated by them, and these practices had developed over the course of time. For instance, the festival of Rakshabandhan was observed by the emperor in a very special way, which had an interesting history. Shah Alam II had symbolically adopted a Hindu woman as his 'sister' after she had guarded the dead body of his father, who had been treacherously murdered. She, and following her death, her descendants, continued to tie rakhis to the emperors right up to the time of Bahadur Shah. On Holi, the swangs (a sort of tableau, usually satirizing people or institutions) created by the city folk would be paraded before the emperor.[136]

Hindu festivals were occasions when special darbars were held in the palace and Hindu courtiers and employees of the emperor presented nazars or offerings and were given honours and gifts in return. The celebration of Dussehra had militaristic connotations, with the horses from the royal stables being ceremonially paraded before the emperor and a hawk being placed on his wrist. On Holi and Diwali, the emperor bathed in the water of seven wells. For Diwali, the palace was specially lit and the emperor sent trays of sweets to his family. There were also some interesting practices associated with this festival. The doors of the mahal inhabited by women were closed to all men for three days, a buffalo was killed at each of the palace gates, and 'meats and bowls of wine and sherbet [were placed] on the bastions of the palace'. There was also giving of alms on festive occasions like Diwali and Holi. The emperor was weighed in different kinds of grain, precious metals, etc. that were then given in charity. This was a practice that was also followed on other occasions like eclipses of the moon.[137]

Most of the Mughal rulers had seen themselves as rulers of all the people of India, irrespective of class and religious belief. Their personal and courtly practices expressed these sentiments. Even at a time when the emperor's financial situation was modest, regular gestures of generosity were expressed. Coins were distributed to crowds of the poor who gathered around the emperor's processions. There are instances of shopkeepers who brought goods for sale to the royal gardens, having their entire stock bought up on the emperor's account. The palace also gave patronage to a variety of performers. Wrestlers, acrobats and actors frequently came into the palace and performed, and were given handsome rewards. Anyone arriving with a hard-luck story—a stranger to the city who had been robbed on his way for instance—was given financial assistance. The generosity extended to the occupants of various royal properties, who would often come and ask for remissions in rent, which were readily granted them by the emperor. The city kotwal was given a present of a hundred and twenty five rupees after the wedding of Bahadur Shah's favourite son,

Jawan Bakht, in recognition of the efficient arrangements made by that officer.[138]

In their turn, the people of Shahjahanabad felt a closeness to the Mughals that they did not quite share with the British, who were the new rulers of the city. They continued to bring announcements of births, marriages and deaths to the emperor. They gave and received gifts on important occasions, and a good many received titles and honours, which they cherished. They also continued to bring their grievances to the emperor, often appearing below the Jharokha, where the emperor still gave darshan. Their petitions usually concerned simple everyday matters. For instance, in 1852, the dhobis of the city gathered under the Jharokha and complained that the deputy magistrate had forbidden them to wash their clothes in the usual place, in the nallah, or stream, from Qudsiya Bagh to the Masjid ghats, and had asked them to cross the river instead. Bahadur Shah reminded them that these were matters of city administration and therefore outside his jurisdiction. They were however so insistent and loud in their complaints that he promised to write a letter to the authorities on the subject.[139]

The East India Company, of course, also had interactions and relationships with the people, if not at the intimate level that characterized a dynasty that had made itself a part of the land over a long duration. In the early years of the Company's rule in Shahjahanabad, their closest allies were those who had helped them defeat the Marathas. These included bankers and merchants like Bhawani Shankar and Har Sukh Rai, who had provided financial assistance during the war. Both were rewarded with jagirs, or revenue-free lands, but these were later reclaimed on the deaths of the grantees.[140] Armed chieftains who had given military support were given hereditary lands, forming a ring of hereditary estates around Delhi. These included Faiz Talab Khan, who was made the nawab of Pataudi, Ahmad Baksh Khan, the nawab of Loharu and Firozpur Jhirka, and Nijabut Ali Khan, the nawab of Jhajjar. All three of them built grand havelis in Shahjahanabad. They spent much of their time in the city, and made up an important part of its elite.[141]

Another strong ally of the British was Begum Samru. In recognition of her support in the wars with the Marathas, her jagir was confirmed by the East India Company. In 1807, Begum Samru purchased a prime piece of land in the heart of the city and built on it a grand house set in a large garden.[142] After her death this building was occupied by the Delhi Bank, and later came to be known as Bhagirath Palace, as it continues to be called today.

An interesting figure of Delhi society in the first half of the nineteenth century was James Skinner, the son of a Scottish military adventurer and an Indian woman. He had been raised as a Muslim, and entered the Maratha army as a mercenary soldier. When war with the East India Company broke out, he was forced out by the Marathas, whose armies were dominated by French mercenaries. He joined the British forces with his troop of soldiers, and gave valuable service. Yet Skinner's position was complicated by his mixed parentage. He was only given a proper commission as a colonel in the British army in

1829, and that, too, after a long struggle. Skinner had an estate in Hansi, but spent a lot of time in Delhi.[143]

Skinner had built a house in Kucha Raiman, south of Chandni Chowk, in 1811, but soon sold this to build another one close to Kashmiri Gate. The part of the city just within the Kashmiri Gate was where many of the higher British officials lived. The palace of Dara Shukoh had been converted into the Residency—where the highest British official in Delhi lived and worked. To this end, it was given a classical European façade, hiding its original Mughal character. Other large mansions, such as that of Ali Mardan Khan, were also similarly converted for the use of other officials. Skinner also built a grand church at Kashmiri Gate, St James', and it was during its consecration in 1836 that he and his three sons were confirmed in their Christian faith.[144]

Skinner's decision to move to this part of the city was prompted by his attempt to fit into British society. Shahjahanabad, just as the rest of India, had in Mughal times been very diverse, not only with regard to the variety of ethnicities that populated it, but also in how open the Mughal administration and army were in giving them employment. Under the rules of the East India Company, the higher echelons of the civil and military administration were open only to Europeans. With the subjugation of the Indian states to British arms, soldiers of mixed parentage, who had been happily accepted in Mughal and Maratha armies, now had no avenues for advancement. This explains James Skinner's attempts to emphasize the British side of his family legacy.

Soldiers of Skinner's Horse regiment. A drawing by John Luard, published in 1838.

Apart from his formal conversion to Christianity, he brought up his children in a Western lifestyle, even sending his son Hercules to England for seven or eight years to receive 'the education of an English gentleman'.[145] Though Skinner had a problem getting a commission in the British army, his troop, Skinner's Horse, was kept on as an 'irregular' regiment in the army. Skinner's Horse is a part of the Indian Army even today.

The cultural concerns of the majority of the educated elite of Shahjahanabad were very different from those of the Skinners. In the early nineteenth century, there were a number of traditional institutions of higher learning, madrasas, some of which, such as that run by Shah Abdul Aziz and his brothers, were of a high standard. The children of the elite, to begin with, usually received an education at home, from an ustani, a lady employed for the purpose. As they advanced further, boys then graduated to a maktab, a more regular primary school, though, in well-off families, teachers were often employed to come to the home. Further education took place at a madrasa, or from other scholars, who were not teachers per se, but were experts in their own fields. It was a tradition that the learned, whatever their full-time occupations, often made it a point to teach students in their spare time. These men would also frequently extend financial help to needy students. In fact, those without means and without connections had a good chance of acquiring a reasonable education if they were determined. We know of several young men who came to Delhi penniless and went on to receive a good education. These included the poet Altaf Husain 'Hali' and the novelist Nazir Ahmad.[146]

By 1825, students from Delhi, or those coming from surrounding areas looking for an education, had an alternative to the older institutions. This was an institution set up by the government—the Delhi College. This was housed in a pre-existing educational establishment—the madrasa of Ghaziuddin Khan, just outside Ajmeri Gate. The aim was that the major part of the curriculum should consist of the study of geography, arithmetic, history, mathematics, mechanics, the use of globes, astronomy, chemistry and other subjects. The medium of instruction obviously had to be one that the pupils readily understood. To this end, it was initially proposed that translations be made in simple Persian from suitable texts, though soon came the realization that Urdu, which was much more widely understood, would be a better choice. The process of translation was slow to take off, and there was a lack of books from which to teach Western sciences. Initially therefore it was the 'oriental' subjects that were primarily taught—for instance, Islamic law. The few areas in which Western ideas were introduced included geography, geometry and the Copernican system of astronomy—at the core of which was the belief that the sun was the centre of the universe.[147]

As regards language, the students learnt either Persian, Arabic or Sanskrit, in that order of popularity. The ultimate aim, however, at least according to the majority official opinion, was to be the introduction of English. In early 1827, Charles Metcalfe, the Resident, declared that the institution of an English professorship would 'be more valuable than all the other arrangements of that institution', and that a familiarity with English would truly open up the stores of European literature and science to the students. Accordingly, in 1828, a class teaching English was also started.[148] The curriculum provided by the Delhi College proved to be quite popular with the people of Shahjahanabad, who were quite open to new ideas. Early in the century Shah Abdul Aziz had pronounced a fatwa that sanctioned Western learning and a study of the English language, as long as it did not conflict with religious belief.[149]

Even outside the college, the citizens of Delhi soon proved to be quite open to the new culture that the advent of the British brought in. An English visitor coming from Calcutta to Delhi in the 1830s went so far as to remark that 'In no other part of our Eastern possessions do the natives shew so earnest a desire to imitate European fashions'. She also noticed that many homes revealed a desire to experiment with European styles of architecture—using 'Grecian piazzas, porticos, and pediments'. She added, 'The shops are crowded with all sorts of European products and manufactures, and many of them display signboards, on which the names and occupations of the inhabitants are emblazoned in Roman characters—a novel circumstance in a native city'. The royal family were second to none in adopting the new fashions. Babar, the son of Akbar II, could often be seen driving about 'in an English chariot drawn by eight horses, in which he frequently appears attired in the full-dress uniform of a British general officer'.[150]

The Delhi College saw its heyday in the 1840s and '50s. In 1844, it moved to what used to be the Residency building, near

Kashmiri Gate. It acquired a good library and a well-equipped laboratory. It was also the centre for the Vernacular Translation Society, which was set up in the early 1840s by the college principal, Felix Boutros, as a response to the needs of the college for appropriate textbooks. Over the next several years it was responsible for the translation of many works, mostly from English, but also from Arabic, Persian and Sanskrit, into Urdu. This involved the efforts of many teachers and senior students of the college.[151]

Though most of those who entered the college aspired for no more than that it would qualify them for a job in the administration, the college was also a vibrant community, that produced many of the new generation of intellectual elite in the city. Mohammad Baqir, who had been a student and then for a short while a teacher in the college, went on to become the editor of the influential Urdu newspaper, the *Dehli Urdu Akhbar*. The newspaper was in the vanguard of social change in the city, taking up issues such as widow remarriage. It also discussed government policies—criticizing the disparity in pay and service conditions between Indian and British functionaries, the imposition of the chowkidari tax (which was a poll tax imposed in 1841), and the government's failure to fix prices of grain in times of scarcity.[152]

Another illustrious student was 'Master' Ram Chander, who went on to become a mathematics teacher in the college. He was particularly committed to the dissemination of Western scientific thought, and was the main force behind two weekly newspapers, which were, in large part, devoted to that objective. These two newspapers, *Muhibb-e-Hind* and *Fawaid-ul-Nazarin*, featured articles on scientific, political and cultural subjects which basically were intended to educate the readers about modern developments in Europe, while at the same time attacking all that was seen as regressive in Indian society. Since Ram Chander was also concerned with making this new knowledge intelligible to Indians in their own tongue, all his writing was in Urdu. He produced original work in his particular field of interest—mathematics—which was aimed at integrating modern Western models with an indigenous idiom. His first book on mathematics, *A Treatise on the Problems of Maxima and Minima*, was published in 1850, and was much acclaimed. It sought to apply the theory of equations, which was a field in which Indians were traditionally considered strong, to the solution of elementary problems of calculus.[153]

Another alumnus of the college, Karimuddin, was actively involved in the translation programme. He also briefly set up his own printing press, rather idealistically named *Rafa-e-Aam*, literally, 'public welfare'. Karimuddin hoped to print inexpensive copies of translations of books for the spread of knowledge among his fellow countrymen. Unfortunately this was a venture that failed, because of Karimuddin's falling out with his partners in the enterprise. Karimuddin also seems to have written some original works, which were pioneering attempts. One, published in 1862 and called *Khat-e-Taqdir*, is believed to be the first novel in Urdu. In it Karimuddin deliberately decided to depart from the qissas, which were popular at the time. Instead of writing on themes of kings, love, fantastic beings and supernatural phenomena, which were characteristic of the qissas, he sought to write a realistic tale, from which people would derive valuable lessons as well as entertainment.[154]

Another work by Karimuddin, produced in the mid-1840s, was essentially a manual for the education of women, entitled *Talim-un-Nissa*. Though Karimuddin mentions it in a list of his works, unfortunately no copies exist and nothing is known of whether it was actually published and circulated, and, if so, whether it was actually read by or to any women. It covered various topics such as the fundamentals of religious belief and practice, and topics of a secular nature, that would help women in their everyday lives such as management of their homes and maintenance of good health. This book is important because it was a precursor to the popular domestic manuals that were to emerge only in the 1880s in Bengal, and in Urdu only in 1905, when Maulana Ashraf Ali Thanawi's *Bahishti Zewar*, a similar work, was published. Inspired by contemporary English domestic manuals aimed at making women more efficient managers of homes, these were adapted to the specific local cultural contexts.[155]

The print media and the college were part of a larger public sphere, within which the people of Delhi engaged in social, cultural and intellectual pursuits. One institution of prominence was the Archaeological Society of Delhi, where a scientific interest in the built heritage of the city was formalized under the aegis of the government. It bore a strongly official character, for it was presided over by the Commissioner and the meetings were held at venues such as the Residency and the Delhi College. Its membership included several British officials and also a significant number of the learned elite of the city. Its secretary was James Cargill, principal of the Delhi College (1850-54); also among the members were Fredrick Taylor, headmaster of the English section of the college, and various Indians—Ziauddin Ahmad Khan, who was the nawab of Ferozepur Jhirka as well as a scholar and poet; Sadruddin Azurda, a scholar and the Principal Sadar Amin (a judicial officer); Rai Ram Saran Das, Deputy Collector; Master Ram Chander; Dr Chiman Lal who was the Sub-Assistant Surgeon; and Syed Ahmad Khan, Munsif (a junior judicial officer).[156]

Syed Ahmad Khan, who went on to become a well-known social and educational reformer, known to us better as 'Sir Syed', was particularly interested in historical and archaeological subjects. He was from an eminent family of Delhi, and his educational career tells us how vibrant the education system, even outside the Delhi College, was. Apart from studying a range of Arabic and Persian texts, he had studied medicine, mathematics and astronomy. While posted at Delhi in the 1840s, he researched and wrote an important book in Urdu—*Asar-us-Sanadid*. This was a description of the history of the several historical cities and many important buildings of Delhi. It also included an account of important contemporaries—hakims, Sufis, musicians and others. This book was very well received and later led to Syed Ahmad being made an Honorary Fellow of the Royal Asiatic Society of Great Britain and Ireland. Syed Ahmad's contributions to the proceedings of the Archaeological Society of Delhi included a detailed scholarly report on the Jantar Mantar, and one on Mehrauli, in which he controversially claimed that the Qutub Minar was built by Rai Pithora, the twelfth-century Rajput ruler.[157]

While the Delhi College and the Archaeological Society represented new institutions and avenues of intellectual endeavour, older traditions still flourished. Delhi continued to be pre-eminent in the field of poetry, and this was the age of Asadullah Khan 'Ghalib', Momin Khan 'Momin', Mohammad Ibrahim 'Zauq', and of course Bahadur Shah 'Zafar', the emperor himself. Though there was some writing in Persian, the popularity of Urdu continued to grow. The mushaira flourished in the early decades of the nineteenth century, as it had in the previous century. Apart from those organized in the palace, mushairas were regularly held at the houses of prominent citizens. One of these was Shah Nasir, the great ustad, whom many poets of the age acknowledged as their teacher. Another was Zafaryab Khan 'Sahab', the son of Walter Reinhardt 'Sombre', who lived in Delhi till the first few years of the century. A series of mushairas was also started at the Delhi College under the initiative of Faiz 'Parsa', a mathematics teacher. These were often memorable occasions and the battles between the ustads went down in history.[158]

From the 1830s onwards there was a proliferation of printing presses, and this contributed to the popular spread of Urdu poetry. Earlier, only those who participated in the exclusive mushairas, or could afford to buy the expensive manuscript books of poetry, had ready access to the poetry of the great ustads. Now books could be produced more cheaply, and more people could afford them. Poetry also found space in practically every newspaper published. Sometimes this was simply a marketing exercise that had very little to do with a personal interest in poetry on the part of the publisher or editor. For instance, we have no evidence that Master Ram Chander took any interest in Urdu poetry, and yet every issue of *Muhibb-e-Hind* printed some poetry, though it was unconnected to the rest of the subject matter of the newspaper. Clearly this was in response to a perceived public demand, and it was hoped that the inclusion of poetry would help to sell the paper.[159]

The increasing dissemination of poetry through the medium of printed books and newspapers also provided guidance and inspiration for a large number of budding poets. We know that more and more people were writing poetry, because the mushairas from the 1840s onwards were not intimate gatherings, but large assemblies. In the Red Fort, the spacious Diwan-e-Aam began to be used for mushairas, and people sat cheek-by-jowl.[160] Also, the tazkiras, or biographical dictionaries of poets, tell us of the hundreds of poets who were writing at the time.

This exciting period of cultural vitality has been referred to as the 'Delhi Renaissance'. It held within it great promise—of showing the way towards a successful adoption of Western advancements in learning, into an education system based on an indigenous language, and co-existing with a long-standing literary tradition. The promise was not to be fulfilled. The whole edifice—including the Delhi College and the Mughal royal court, was to be swept away in 1857.

A newspaper illustration of the skirmish in front of St James' Church on 11 May 1857.

The Revolt and its Aftermath

ON 11 MAY 1857, THE CITY AWAKENED TO WHAT, AT FIRST, appeared to be a minor excitement. This was the arrival of a troop of soldiers who had mutinied the previous evening at Meerut. They had made their way to Delhi with the intention of starting a rebellion under the leadership of the Mughal emperor, who still was, for the population at large, a symbol of sovereignty, though a hollow one. The mutineers received active help from troops stationed in Delhi, who were inspired to mutiny against their officers, and also from some of the people of the city. Their immediate move was to declare Bahadur Shah their sovereign, and to take full control of the city. The emperor was slow to fall in with their plan but, in time, more or less accepted the *fait accompli*. The aim of ridding the city of British control was accomplished, in large part, by physically eliminating all British officials that could be found. An equally harsh line was taken against those who were perceived as being their natural allies—Europeans in semi-public or private positions, such as the principal of the Delhi College and the manager of the Delhi Bank, women and children of these officials and other men, and even some Indian Christians.

Not surprisingly, one of the first results of the arrival of mutinous troops in Delhi was disorder. In the wake of the terror unleashed against those whom the soldiers perceived as the enemy, came a frenzy of looting. In this a major part was played by another category of outsiders. On their way from Meerut to Delhi the mutineers had collected around them convicts from the Meerut jail and people from the villages surrounding Delhi, mostly Gujjars. These were people who looked on a military excursion as an opportunity to indulge in looting. This they proceeded to do in the next few days—targeting shops and also some houses, particularly those of Europeans, bankers and merchants. They were soon joined by some of the population of the city. The *Dehli Urdu Akhbar* reported that on 11 May, as the soldiers went through the city chasing the British officers, in their wake were the 'common people' of the city, armed with whatever came to hand—a piece of wood, a stick of bamboo, or even the leg of a bed. They were the ones who told the soldiers which were the houses of the Europeans, and of those Indians who were supposedly friendly with them. Many of these were killed.[161]

The soldiers, of course, wanted to eliminate all potential sources of opposition. But the people of Delhi had mixed motivations. Some amount of pure vindictiveness against symbols of colonial rule and culture is evident, for instance in the wanton destruction of the Delhi College, its library and laboratory, and the ripping up of English books.[162] But there were other motives, too. A major source of support for the mutineers in Delhi, were the poor and the marginalized, a 'turbulent' population that had always been a potential source of trouble. They evidently saw this as an opportunity to create disorder and rob their neighbours. On their arrival, the soldiers had immediately released the prisoners from the kotwali, and these men are likely to have been among the so-called 'scum of the population', that was seen 'hurrying to and fro, laden with the plunder of European houses'. One eyewitness of the events of that day saw a large group of pahalwans, wrestlers, on the street. On the one hand, they attacked government property—one breaking a street lamp, exclaiming, 'there goes another kafir (unbeliever)', but on the other, also tried to break open locks on shops.[163]

Over the next four months, a formal administration was set up in the city, with Bahadur Shah as its nominal head. All orders of the administration were in his name, and some of the royal princes were given military appointments. For a while the emperor's son, Mirza Mughal, was also made commander-in-chief. Yet, actual power was in the hands of a council of soldier-leaders. Though they saw the utility of using the emperor's name and influence to lend legitimacy to their authority, the soldiers often did not treat him with respect. Some of the officers addressed Bahadur Shah as *'arrey Badsha'* (You! Emperor!) or *'arrey buddha'* (You! Old man!) and took the ultimate liberty of touching his hand and beard.[164]

Nevertheless, Bahadur Shah's major concern was not for his own safety and dignity. On the very first day, he remonstrated with the troops killing British officials but received the reply, 'it appears you are in league with the Christians—you will see what will happen'. He argued with the soldiers who wanted to take the lives of a large group of Europeans who had been imprisoned by the soldiers in the palace, but to no effect. A church organist and his son were hidden by the royal consort, Zinat Mahal, in her house, but when trying to leave the city some days later, were shot.[165]

Bahadur Shah was also sympathetic to the sufferings of the people of the city. As the revolt broke out in the surrounding territories, and ultimately through most of North and Central India, large numbers of soldiers and freelance rebels started converging on Delhi. They arrived in Delhi looking for leadership and support, but their influx put a great strain on the city since, at their peak in late July, they numbered some 50,000. Though many of these troops brought treasure with them, and attempts were also made to gather land revenue from surrounding areas, more money and provisions were required to keep the campaign going. The earliest requisitions in the city were from traders, bankers and shopkeepers, and they were as a rule extremely reluctant to oblige, even on the understanding that anything advanced in cash or kind would be treated strictly as a loan. As the days progressed, the condition worsened. In the first half of June, the British returned with reinforcements and established themselves on the Ridge overlooking the city. This resulted in constant military engagements and increased the needs of the army. As the soldiers began to face serious shortages, pressure began to be put on wealthy citizens to make contributions. The result of this appeal was not encouraging, and by mid-August these people were being threatened with imprisonment if they did not pay up.[166]

Lesser individuals also suffered because the need to support a large body of troops put a general strain on the city. The soldiers needed lodging, food, fuel, construction supplies for military works, and so on, and their attempts to procure these led to many of the 'excesses' they were accused of. The soldiers camped wherever they found space, inconveniencing the people of the city. The tenants of the shops of Chandni Chowk began to leave because the soldiers had stationed their horses in the open square. The palace was not immune to encroachments either. Bahadur Shah regularly complained, to no avail, of the soldiers who were camping in his gardens within the fort. The residents of the city also suffered from shortages and high prices of essentials, caused by the obstructions the conflict placed in the way of a free flow of goods, and by hoarders who pushed up prices. The poor had only their labour to offer, and this was often forcibly requisitioned for the military, particularly towards the end of August and September, when there was no money to pay for labour. Finally, of course, people regularly died of the hazards of war—from cannon shot from British lines outside the wall, and from accidents such as an explosion in the gunpowder factory.[167]

What sustained the revolt in Delhi, until the military defeat in mid-September, was a strong anti-British feeling. This was often expressed in terms of religion, and the rebels frequently described their struggle as 'fighting for one's religion'. However, apart from the customary mention of the 'defence of faith' that prefaced many orders and letters, the more detailed proclamations issued by the rebel government at Delhi, in fact, talked primarily of economic grievances. These included raised revenue rates, chowkidari tax, the lack of employment for respectable and learned men, toll on the use of roads, etc. The threat to religion was mentioned but was, by no means, the only or even the most prominent factor.[168]

Some of the most well-articulated criticism of British rule can be seen in the pages of the *Dehli Urdu Akhbar* during those months. On 21 June 1857, it reminded its readers that, during their rule, the British had given all higher government jobs, worth hundreds of rupees a month, to people of their own colour. Besides this, they spent money very carefully and lived frugally. As a result, they saved thousands and lakhs of rupees and took this money to their country. Thus, their wealth did not spread in our country and their gold and property did not bring any benefits to our people.[169] This is a remarkably clear early expression of the drain of wealth theory, which is usually associated with the nationalist economist Dadabhai Naoroji's writings of a decade later.

The idea that the Mughal dynasty, in contrast to the British, had been more sympathetic to the people, was a major justification for revolt in its name. In the issue of the newspaper dated 14 June, a long article pointed out that the Mughal dynasty had not discriminated between its subjects on the basis of religion, and had allowed all to follow their own inclinations. This was in sharp contrast to the British—'who during an unbroken rule of a hundred years referred to creatures of God as "vile" and to your brothers and kin as "black man!", "black man!" and thus dishonoured and disgraced them'.[170] The racism associated with British rule was a deeply felt reality.

While these anti-British feelings tied the people together in revolt, the idea of nationalism did not, as yet, exist. Its seeds, however, can be found in some of the declarations of the administration. A proclamation issued in the name of the emperor on 6 September 1857, illustrates the fact that the revolt sought to unite people on a basis that transcended religion and ethnicity. It read:

> This is a religious war, and is being prosecuted on account of the faith and that it behoves all Hindoos and Mussulman residents of the Imperial city, whether they be men of the Eastern Provinces or Seikhs or foreigners [it is likely that the original here was *wilayati*, commonly used for Afghans] or natives of the Himalaya hills or Nepaulese…whenever they come over to this side…they will be allowed to continue in their own creed and religions.[171]

The emperor as well as the council of soldiers took great pains to ensure religious harmony in the city, and were, by and large, successful. Though, from time to time, there were issues and disputes that cropped up, the situation was generally diffused by timely action. Bahadur Shah issued frequent proclamations in the city urging Hindus and Muslims to maintain peace between each other. As Eid approached, he also instituted a ban on cow slaughter to maintain peace in the city, and the festival passed off peacefully.[172]

The fault-lines in the city lay elsewhere. The soldiers controlling the administration were an alien element, mostly drawn from the peasantry of the Eastern Doab. The elite of Delhi in particular looked upon these 'Purabias' (easterners), as they were commonly called, with suspicion, and even revulsion. This feeling comes across in some of the poetry that was written immediately after the revolt. The typical *Dehliwala*'s cultural chauvinism comes to the fore in many descriptions.

The poet Mirza Khan 'Dagh' wrote:

Jagah jagah the zamindar dar ki surat
chadhe hi ate the sar par bukhar ki surat
bala se kam na thi ek ek ganwar ki surat

Everywhere there were peasants like gibbets (death)
They were irrepressible, like a fever
Each rustic had the face of evil

Ghazab mein koi jo raiyat, bala mein shahar aya
yeh purbi nahin aye, khuda ka kahar aya,

The raging peasants entered the city as an evil
The wrath of God arrived in the form of these easterners[173]

It was not only the alien soldiers that the elite were suspicious of. The poor enjoyed a social revolution of sorts during the four months of the revolt. The account of Zahir Dehlavi, a young man who wrote a memoir of those days, tells us, in somewhat more detail than others, about the people represented in the so-called 'mob'. There were criminals such as pickpockets and thieves, but there were also various other occupational groups such as wrestlers, tanners, manual scavengers, washermen, water carriers, butchers, greengrocers, and weavers. They were said to have joined in the looting, often collecting large amounts of money, such as when the Delhi Bank was attacked. The circumstance of war also provided them a chance for upward mobility, as some used their newfound wealth to buy horses and weapons and thus join the fighting men. A mob often also followed closely behind troops as they went out of the city walls to attack enemy troops, hoping to mop up plunder from the latter's camp. The role of the mob was not entirely negative either. It was said that it was the city badmashes who constantly exhorted the soldiers to get down to the task of defeating the enemy, chaffing them on signs of hesitance and accusing them of cowardice.[174]

The propertied classes in general, whatever their views on British rule, were unsettled by the spectacle of social revolution, which they could see unfolding before their eyes. It was not simply a case of temporary 'disorders' and inconveniences caused by war. They saw control slipping into the hands of alien peasant soldiers, and the lower classes of the city. They were not convinced that, when British rule was uprooted completely, power would be in the hands of the emperor, the soldiers would melt away, the labouring poor would take up their occupations quietly and things would be otherwise back to normal. These fears come out most explicitly in the poems that were written as a lament, soon after the revolt.

Zahir Dehlavi wrote of how the 'riff-raff' joined the soldiers in creating disorder in the city:

Jahan mein jitne the aubash rind nafarjam
daghasha'air chughalkhor badmash tamam
hue sharik e sipah e sharir o badanjam
kiya tamam sharifon ke nam ko badnam

The world's rakes and rogues, the insignificant
All cheats, slanderers, and rascals
Became partners with the wicked soldiers who were destined for a bad end
They maligned the good name of all respectable people.[175]

A strong sense of an upturning of the social order is evident in some of the poetry. Mohammad Zahur 'Zahur' wrote:

Sada tanur jhonke tha jo ladka nanbai ka
bhara hai is ke sar mein ab to sauda mirzai ka
qaroli bandh kar nikle hai ab ladka qasai ka
amiron ke barabar baithe hai farzand dai ka

The street cook's lad, who did nothing but stoke the fire,
Now he fancies himself a mirza
The son of the butcher goes around wearing a hunting knife
The son of the midwife sits on level with noblemen.[176]

It was for these reasons that many of the elite of the city began to withdraw their support from the revolt. A few actively connived with British spies, but mostly it was their reluctance to offer financial support that weakened the war effort. Though the rebel soldiers, suddenly freed of their highest leadership (the British officers), often lacked organization and discipline, they were not short of courage and the British got a much stiffer fight than they had expected. Nevertheless, engagements with the enemy usually took a very heavy toll of both armies, with hundreds of soldiers sometimes being killed and an equal number wounded, on a single occasion. This, along with shortages of ammunition, delays in pay, the frequent disagreements and rivalry between the regiments and their officers, mutual suspicions of betrayal to the enemy, led, eventually, to an erosion of morale on the Indian side. Soon they were facing repeated defeats against the British, who had meanwhile strengthened their position.[177]

By August, the possibility of defeat was a real one, and the soldiers began to leave the city to carry on the fight in other theatres in India. At the end of August, it was estimated that less than five thousand rebel soldiers were left in the city. The British force blew open Kashmiri Gate and entered Shahjahanabad on 14 September. Bahadur Shah, accompanied by several members of his family, left to take shelter in Humayun's tomb. Some of the townspeople, together with such soldiers as had not left, fought hard to hold out in the streets of the city for a while, until on the 20th, the entire city and the fort had been overcome.[178]

Not for the first time in its history, the city witnessed a bloodbath. Dead bodies piled up in the streets, causing a horrific stench of decomposition. As a result, cholera soon broke out. Such of the inhabitants as had not left their homes of their own accord, were driven out. Large numbers of people hung about outside the city walls and faced starvation, disease and lack of shelter and clothing. Some took shelter in the ruins surrounding the city, including Humayun's tomb and the Qutub. Even in these places they were not safe, for passing British troops would drive them away, leaving them, according to one British official, 'scattered all over the country and in the greatest misery'.[179]

The rich, who had withheld their property from the soldiers, were now to lose it to the looting invaders. Apart from a desire to possess themselves of valuables, there was also a spirit of destruction that filled the invading soldiery in the first few days of the takeover. Walls and floors of houses were broken in search of hidden valuables; furniture and mirrors were smashed. Whole libraries of Persian and Arabic books were deliberately destroyed. Soon after, official Prize Agents were appointed by the army to appropriate enemy property in a more systematic manner. Vast amounts of property, both movable and immovable, was confiscated.[180]

Bahadur Shah had agreed to a peaceful surrender on the condition that his life would be spared. He was brought back to Shahjahanabad and imprisoned in the fort. Major Hodson, in charge of transporting three princes (two sons and a grandson of Bahadur Shah) from Humayun's tomb, shot them near Delhi Gate in cold blood, and brought their bodies back to the kotwali in the heart of the city, to be publicly exposed. Bahadur Shah was tried by a military commission, which found him guilty of conspiracy, rebellion and waging war against the government. The doubtful question of whether he could, at all, be considered a subject of the government, was not addressed. Following the trial, it was decided that Bahadur Shah, his wife Zinat Mahal, and sons Jawan Bakht and Shah Abbas would be exiled to Rangoon.[181]

Many other prominent leaders of the rebellion were tried and executed. According to one official report, some five hundred men were 'disposed of summarily' in the early months after the capture of Delhi. Another fifteen hundred or so were awaiting trial and their numbers were increasing as more arrests were made. By the end of 1857 several hundred had been hanged in Delhi. The British soldiers 'bribed the executioner to keep them a long time hanging, as they liked to

The surrender of Bahadur Shah Zafar. An illustration from a history book published in 1858.

see the criminals dance a "Pandies' hornpipe", as they termed the dying struggles of the wretches'. Many male members of the royal family were also executed. Many more were exiled to farflung places—mostly in Burma and to Karachi.[182]

Probably much longer was the list of the people who were shot, mostly in cold blood, without the benefit of a trial at all. Vivid reminders of the immediate horrors stayed in Delhi for months—the two gallows in Chandni Chowk, the pervading nauseous smell, and the ruined houses. And yet, amidst this desolation, the main street of Chandni Chowk was an incongruous spectacle of bustle, and brisk business in all manner of goods, a large portion of it loot. It was all for the benefit of the many British soldiers, officers and their families who were now living in the better houses in the city and in the fort, and also, to some extent, for the Sikh and Gurkha soldiers stationed at or passing through Delhi.[183]

Meanwhile, most of the people of the city were still outside the walls. The policy was one that discriminated on the basis of religion. The British had decided that the blame for the revolt was to be laid at the door of Muslims in general. So, though in the beginning of 1858, Hindus were given permission to return, Muslims were kept out for much longer. They were given passes to enter the city for specific purposes, but could not reoccupy their houses or otherwise take up residence in the city till late in 1859. By that time, many had given up hope and started new lives elsewhere. The population within the city walls, which had been over 137,000 before the Revolt, was down to about 102,332 in 1864. More significantly, the number of Muslims had fallen to 39,434, and that of Hindus and Jains to 61,324, a decrease of 40 and 14 per cent respectively. The population did not recover to pre-Revolt levels till the end of the century.[184]

The physical map of the city was affected in the aftermath of the suppression of the revolt. The immediate imperative was a military one. The defences of Delhi had to be destroyed, its fortifications, walls and gates rendered useless for defence. Most of the buildings within the Red Fort were destroyed. To make the task easier, since many of the buildings were made of stone, explosives were used.[185] Some of the ground was subsequently covered with military buildings—the most prominent being tall barracks.

Many buildings of the city were demolished as well. This was justified on the grounds of security requirements, namely, that an area five hundred yards in width, of shooting distance, be cleared around the fort. Ultimately, the clearance stopped just short of four hundred and fifty yards, so that Dariba would be spared. This was done on the application of the tradesmen of that important business hub. Many important localities and buildings were sacrificed to the clearances, including the Akbarabadi mosque. Some of the important property that was destroyed in other parts of the city had belonged to the members of the royal family. This included Jahanara's sarai and the hammam in Chandni Chowk. Much of Daryaganj was cleared, and troops were stationed there.

An important part of the punishment meted out to the Muslims of the city specifically, was the occupation of the

Eidgah, the Jama Masjid, the Fatehpuri Masjid and the Zinat-ul-Masjid. The quadrangle and arcades of the Fatehpuri Masjid were auctioned, and bought by one of the richest banker-merchants of Delhi, Lala Chunna Mal. The Zinat-ul-Masjid became a bakery for the army. There was a significant turnover in ownership of commercial and residential property too. A large amount of property, belonging to those found guilty of rebellion, had been confiscated. A part of this was gifted to those who had served the British loyally during the revolt. Much of it ended up in the hands of a few rich traders who had liquid cash to buy up property that was going cheap.[186]

Dagh wrote a ghazal that contains a highly ironic account of the new British order in the city:

> *Muzhda ai bakht, ke phir aye yahan sahib log*
> *zeb e dehli hai koi, koi hai shan e dehli*
> *De diye fauj ko hukkam ne inam mein sab*
> *ganj kavon se fuzun ganj e nihan e dehli*
> *Qile mein barakein lohe ki bani hain kya khub*
> *nahin kalkatta ab gharz to basan e dehli*

> Glad tidings, O fortune! The sahibs are back;
> One is the ornament of Delhi, one is the glory of Delhi.
> The authorities have given them all to the army as a prize,
> Swarming with diggers are the hidden treasures of Delhi.
> What wonderful concrete barracks in the fort!
> Now Calcutta is not a patch on Delhi.[187]

At the end of 1862, the Jama Masjid was handed over to a committee elected by the majority of the Muslim inhabitants, but they were made to sign an agreement which, among other duties, required them to report any use of seditious language. The rules to be enforced in the mosque were also set down by government, included the clause that 'European officers and gentlemen civil and military can enter without restriction as to shoes'.[188] The Red Fort was now occupied by the army, and lived in by many British officials and their families. Indians could enter only by paying a fee, and were let in to attend the gora bazaars, which were events modelled on the meena bazaars, or women's bazaars, of Mughal times.[189]

The city was slowly rebuilt along new lines. On the northern side of Chandni Chowk, in the place where Jahanara's sarai had stood, the Town Hall was built between 1860-65, out of provincial funds and subscriptions. It was originally known as the Lawrence Institute, after John Lawrence, the Lieutenant Governor of Punjab Province. It housed a chamber of commerce, literary society and museum. In 1866, it was bought over by the Municipality and became the Town Hall. The garden north of Chandni Chowk was re-landscaped and renamed Queen's Garden. It included a cricket ground, a bandstand, and a menagerie containing various animal species. South of it, in the middle of Chandni Chowk, a Clock Tower was built. The Mughal-era hammam had been demolished, and where it had stood, was now one end of a new road, officially named Egerton Road, but popularly called 'Nai Sarak'. In the Kotwali Chowk, a new fountain was built—the phawwara, which in time led to the square being popularly called phawwara chowk or fountain chowk.[190] The channel of water that had flowed along the middle of the street was bricked over.

The railways came to Delhi, the first train steaming in on New Year's Eve 1867. The railway line was built across the northern half of the city, cutting the city in two. It necessitated the demolition of many houses, the owners of which were compensated with property confiscated after the Revolt. The railways had a positive impact on the trade passing through Delhi. Prosperity increased, at least among the trading class. Between 1868 and 1869, the total tax collected from the bankers, piece goods merchants, grain merchants and traders in food in Delhi District, doubled.[191]

That some of the gaiety had returned to the city was noted by a visitor from Calcutta in 1866—Bholanath Chander. He visited Shahjahanabad during Diwali, and noted the 'illumination, and the exhibition of dolls, toys and confectionary' and the 'whole street lighted up by little glass lamps, cherags, and candles'. He also remarked that the 'Mahomedans now fully enjoy the Hindoo festival', though in the mistaken belief that at one time they had not.[192]

While the traders had prospered, the old, mainly Muslim, aristocracy had been impoverished. Many were reduced to manual work, or poorly paid jobs as schoolteachers. Many of them, along with the other poorer population lived on the fringes of the city along the city walls—Mori Gate, Ajmeri Gate, Turkman Gate, Delhi Gate and Khidki Farrashkhana. Former noblewomen were reduced to spinning gota for a subsistence. Famines in the 1860s further compounded the problem by pushing up food prices.[193]

After the revolt, the city had been placed under martial law. In 1861, it came back to civil administration, but under the Punjab Province rather than the North-Western Provinces, to which it had earlier belonged. The Municipality, inaugurated in 1863, became an important agency for the civil management of the city. Not surprisingly, the Municipal Commissioners were mostly members of the mercantile elite—prominent Hindu and Jain merchants, who had supported the British cause during the Revolt. Among the few Muslim members of the municipality was Mirza Illahi Baksh, a member of the royal family, who had covertly helped the British during 1857, and his son. The Municipal council was essentially a conservative body with a limited role; through the 1860s, 75 per cent of Municipal expenditure was spent on the police.[194]

Politically, the decade following the revolt saw quietude. This was not surprising, given the brutality with which the recent revolt had been crushed. Despite the lifting of martial law, there was an overbearing military presence within the city. This was painfully apparent in the large number of guns that were mounted for decades later on the battlements of the Red Fort, directed towards the city as well as towards all external approaches. A sign of the political conservatism that prevailed was a declaration in 1872 by one Nabi Baksh, a member of the Mughal royal family, supported by twelve maulvis, to the effect that jihad against British rule was not lawful.[195]

From the second half of the 1860s however, there were the first stirrings of public debate and questioning of public policies. Much of this was in the press, which rapidly grew in Delhi—from two newspapers in 1866, to fifteen a decade later. Articles appeared from time to time deploring the economic evils of colonial rule, and the exclusion of Indians from any significant administrative role. Another forum for debate was the Delhi Literary Society. Established in 1865, with the stated objectives of 'the advancement of knowledge and general welfare' it consisted of seventeen Englishmen and seventy-six Indians. In its early years largely a forum where 'respectable' gentlemen met to read learned papers and discuss some social issues such as British racial prejudice, it increasingly played a role in representing public grievances to the authorities.[196]

The 1860s-70s was a time when a number of schools, including girls' schools, were opened with the efforts of both Hindus and Muslims. The Anglo-Arabic School was set up in 1872, and was housed in Ghaziuddin Madrasa from 1889. The Anglo-Sanskrit School was established in 1869, in a haveli donated by Lala Chunna Mal near Katra Neel in Chandni Chowk and financed by him. The Delhi College had been reduced to the status of a high school after the revolt, which it remained till 1864, when college level classes were started. The college, though it had not recovered from the damage done to its library and laboratories during 1857, still enjoyed a good reputation. It therefore came as a shock when, in 1877, the government announced that the college classes would be shifted to the Lahore College.[197]

Ironically this announcement was made in the wake of the Imperial Assemblage, or Durbar of 1877, held at Delhi, by which it was hoped to show the British sovereign's 'interest in this great Dependency of Her Crown, and Her Royal confidence in the loyalty and affection of the Princes and People of India'.[198] The nationalist leader Surendranath Banerjea publicly denounced the government, for not being willing to 'spend Rs 12,000 a year for the maintenance of an ancient and time-honoured seat of learning (when) the Delhi Assemblage cost 60 lacs'.[199]

The Imperial Assemblage was designed to be an occasion to celebrate the assumption by Queen Victoria of the title 'Kaiser-e-Hind', 'Empress of India'. The choice of Delhi—far from Calcutta, which was the capital of the British in India, was carefully calculated. As the Viceroy Lytton remarked, it was with the view to 'place the Queen's authority upon the ancient throne of the Moguls, with which the imagination and tradition of [our] Indian subjects associate the splendour of supreme power'.[200] Of the 84,000 people who converged on Delhi for the occasion, were sixty-three ruling princes, and some three hundred 'titular chiefs and native gentlemen' from the vast territories over which the British Indian government either exercised paramountcy or ruled directly.[201]

The Assemblage was held north of the city, in a large space of land between the ridge and the river. The events, spread over two weeks, opened with a ceremonial procession in which the Viceroy and Lady Lytton, seated atop a large elephant on a silver howdah, made their way from the railway station down Chandni Chowk street to the Red Fort, and circling the Jama Masjid, to the imperial camp. The main event—the reading of Queen Victoria's proclamation, took place in a large amphitheatre, presided over by the Viceroy.[202]

The pomp and ornament was designed to appeal to a perceived Indian love of show. As Lytton patronizingly remarked, 'the further East you go, the greater becomes the importance of a bit of bunting'.[203] The attempt to imbue this show with explicitly British symbols, resulted in a particularly tasteless effect. Val C. Prinsep, the British artist who had been commissioned to execute an official painting of the Durbar, found his artistic sensibilities offended by the amphitheatre that had been designed for the main ceremony. He commented, 'Oh horror! What have I to paint? A kind of thing that outdoes the Crystal Palace in "hideosity"…all iron, gold, red, blue and white…The Viceroy's dais is a kind of scarlet temple 80 feet high. Never was there such Brummagem ornament, or more atrocious taste…They have stuck pieces of needlework into stone panels and tin shields and battleaxes all over the place. The size…gives it a vast appearance like a gigantic circus and the decorations are in keeping'.[204]

For Prinsep, this tasteless show appeared to represent the nature of British rule itself. Visiting Jama Masjid, and being moved by its beauty and grandeur, he remarked that for the Durbar site, the government 'could have chosen the front of the Jumma Musjid, about forty steps rising to a magnificent plateau, which overlooks a wide maidan or plain, backed by the ancient fort containing the palace of the old Mogul Emperors. From this position the Viceroy could indeed declare the commencement of the new "Raj"! but the Anglo-Indian

A colourful scene of the Durbar of 1877, from the official history of the event.

has chosen a bare plain, and builds his Brummagem dais with no surroundings or any historical associations. Well, perhaps it is a type of the new Raj—this dais—cold, new, flaunting and bare, without a rag of sentiment or beauty'.[205]

For the people of Shahjahanabad, the Durbar had limited meaning. The Durbar site was well outside the city walls. Even during the Viceroy's one procession through the city, the streets were lined by soldiers, who effectively insulated the cavalcade from the people. As a concession to the people of Delhi, two mosques, the Zinat-ul-Masjid and the Fatehpuri Masjid, which had been confiscated after the revolt, were reopened for worship. An indirect effect of the Durbar was that it drew to Delhi people who would have a long-term effect on the city. Dayanand Saraswati, the founder of the Hindu reform movement, the Arya Samaj, visited Delhi for the Durbar. As a direct outcome of the visit, a branch of the Samaj was formed here the following year. Around the same time, a branch of the Theosophical Society, a neo-Hindu movement, too, was established.[206]

From the second half of the 1870s, there began a phase of increased sectarian activity and conflict. Active proselytization, based on public preaching at bazaars by Christian missionaries, had been going on since soon after the Revolt. Soon, there was a mushrooming of sectarian organizations. Apart from the new movements such as the Theosophical Society and the Arya Samaj, orthodox Hinduism was represented by the establishment of the headquarters of the Bharat Dharam Mahamandal, and the Sanatan Dharam Sabha in the 1890s.

There was also a host of purely local Hindu bodies that sprang up in the 1880s and '90s, many of which were caste-based. In 1878 a Jain Sabha was set up in Dharampura locality, adjoining Dariba, presumably as a response to the Arya Samaj. Among the Muslims, the Anjuman-e-Islamia, founded in 1875, performed the role of promoting the interests of Muslims.[207]

The negative side of the increasing assertion of religious identity were sectarian riots. These conflicts afflicted the city on several occasions during the 1880s and '90s, and centred around issues such as cow-protection and rival religious processions. The latter included conflict between Jains and Hindus. The issue of proselytization and conversion also caused conflict between Christian missionaries, Muslims, Arya Samajis and Sanatan Hindus.[208]

The constructive outcome of these sectarian movements was the founding of educational institutions. Two among these stand out in particular. St Stephen's College was founded in 1881 by the Cambridge Mission. With humble beginnings in a haveli just off Kinari Bazaar, it soon got a new building near Kashmiri Gate. In 1899 the Hindu College was established to provide an education on Sanatanist Hindu lines. The college received financial backing from Kishen Das Gurwala, and was set up in Kinari Bazaar. Then Lala Sultan Singh sold some property in Kashmiri Gate to the college, and it came to occupy a spot just across the road from St Stephen's.[209]

Despite religious disputes that cropped up from time to time, the people of Delhi were able to overcome their differences in times of greater trouble. The famine of 1898-

1900 and the subsequent plague scare brought various communities together, and this solidarity was expressed by Hindus greeting Muslims emerging from the Jama Masjid after Eid, members of the two communities accepting water from each other, and Muslims participating in Holi celebrations.[210]

The Circuit House, transformed into the Viceroy's residence.
Published around 1910.

Shahjahanabad in the Twentieth Century

THE DAWN OF A NEW CENTURY SAW SHAHJAHANABAD POISED on the verge of fundamental changes. In the course of the next half-century, it would go from being a relic of the Mughal empire, to the capital of the British Raj, and soon after, to being relegated to the status of a poor adjunct to the brand new city of New Delhi.

The death of Queen Victoria in 1901 was commemorated in Delhi with the formation of a fund, to which many citizens, particularly those of a loyalist bent, subscribed. The money raised was used to found the Victoria Zanana Hospital (now Kasturba Hospital)—a hospital exclusively for women.[211]

But the death of the 'Empress of India' coincided with the end of an era dominated by loyalists. The new century would see a considerable increase in political activism in the city. In Delhi, the response to the Indian National Congress, which had held its first session in Bombay in December 1885, had been moderate in the late 1880s, and very lukewarm in the 1890s.[212] Soon however the people of Delhi would join nationalist politics in larger numbers.

One of the first organized platforms for protest was the Ratepayers' Association, formed in 1902 to agitate against the House Tax, which had been recently instituted. This was later renamed as the Citizens' Union and began to concern itself with various grievances against municipal and other authorities. This, and a couple of other organizations, became the forum for discussing issues of all-India as well as local importance. The membership consisted mainly of members of the legal profession and St Stephen's College. In 1884, self-government had come to Delhi, in the form of elections to the municipality, based on a restricted ballot. In the 1900s, an increasing number of lawyers began to be elected. This was an important sign of the times. Earlier, members had been almost exclusively bankers and merchants—who were traditionally more conservative.[213]

The Imperial government at Calcutta, however, was still running in its old groove. It was decided that the best way to ensure the loyalty of the Indian people was another Durbar at Delhi, to be held at the end of 1902-early 1903, to announce the coronation of the new monarch, Edward VII. Though many parts of the country were still reeling under the effects of the famines of 1897 and 1900, in which millions had died, the festivities were organized on an unprecedented scale. The viceroy, Curzon, had taken a keen personal interest in the planning of the Durbar, and on his orders, parts of the Red Fort were used for the festivities. The Diwan-e-Aam was renovated and fitted with electric lights, and a Royal tea was held in the Hayat Baksh Bagh.[214]

The Diwan-e-Aam fitted with electric lights for the Durbar of 1903.
From the official souvenir.

Months before the Durbar took place, elaborate construction schemes were underway to prepare the vast camp that accommodated the guests. A veritable tented city had been created, which included a light railway and electric lighting.[215] This was in stark contrast with civic amenities in Shahjahanabad, which tended to lag behind even other Indian cities. A waterworks scheme had only been introduced to the city in the 1890s, after much bickering over the expense involved. Modern drainage would only be completed in 1909. Electricity came to Delhi with the Durbar in 1902, but at first would be used only in industry.[216] The telephone lay somewhat in the future; the first manual telephone exchange was set up in Civil Lines in 1911, and one was added in the Kashmiri Gate area in 1923. [217]

The procession of the Viceroy through the city was grander than it had been in the Durbar of 1877. Unlike the latter, it included the glittering spectacle of the ruling chiefs who had come to the city to attend the assemblage. They joined the procession, seated on their richly caparisoned elephants, accompanied by colourful entourages. Foreign guests and journalists watched the procession from the Jama Masjid, others from the fort. Most Indians, visitors as well as the residents of the city, watched from along the streets, behind a cordon of military guards. More than the Durbar of 1877, the 1903 Durbar was meant to impress the world. The large number of foreign journalists and photographers attending, succeed in conveying this.[218]

Though the world was suitably impressed, none more so

than Britons in India and at home, Indians received the Durbar fairly coldly. There was no gathering of thinkers and leaders, as there had been during the Durbar of 1877, which had brought Dayanand Saraswati and others to the city. During the winter of 1902-3 many of the leaders of Indian civil society were busy with the session of the Indian National Congress, then being held at Ahmedabad. In Delhi, the Indians in the audience received the viceregal procession with an apparent impassivity and silence that surprised European observers. According to one journalist : 'A European was struck by the absence of the enthusiasm which in the West sends people frantic... The cheers were led by the Europeans in the crowd of onlookers, and the East sat and watched.' Though the standard explanation given for this was that 'the native never cheers',[219] this was far from the case. Less than a hundred years before, the British Resident at Delhi had noted that on the occasion of Eid, the emperor's 'elephant passed through the streets of Delhi amidst the acclamations of the multitudes with which they were crowded' [and heard]...the shouts of blessings to which the appearance [of the emperor] gave rise'.[220]

One part of the Durbar that might have been visited by the people of Delhi was an exhibition of Indian handicrafts. This had been organized in Qudsiya Bagh, the garden just outside the Kashmiri Gate. This housed a collection of crafts from all over the country, displayed partly in especially constructed buildings, and at least one pre-existing Mughal pavilion, which had been modified.[221] It was an early example of the trade and crafts exhibitions that are a feature of Delhi today.

Whatever Curzon had been hoping to achieve from the Durbar, by way of mustering support for the British Raj, came to naught just two years later. Seeking to sabotage the growing nationalist movement in Bengal, in 1905 the government announced the partition of the province along communal lines. This immediately led to an outcry and the launch of mass popular protest—the Swadeshi movement, with the boycott of foreign goods as its rallying call. The movement, which began in Bengal, soon spread to other parts of the country, and moved beyond the demand for reversing the partition of Bengal. The December 1906 Calcutta session of the Congress proclaimed the goal of Swaraj, or self-government.[222]

Delhi, too, was affected by the mood of the nation, and there was increased nationalist activity in the period 1906-08. A Swadeshi society, by the name of Sanat-o-Hirfat-Anjuman, was formed and called for the boycott of foreign goods. The only effective boycott, however, was that of the tramway, which had been only recently opened, and connected Jama Masjid, Chandni Chowk, the railway station and the Sabzi Mandi, which lay to the west outside the city walls. The boycott of this clearly did not unduly inconvenience anyone.[223]

At the forefront of nationalist activity in Delhi were Syed Haidar Raza, who had been a student, and for a while a lecturer at St Stephen's College; Prof Raghbar Dayal, also of St Stephen's College; and Lala Amir Chand, a teacher in St Stephen's School. They enjoyed a strong following among the students of the college, of whom a large number enrolled in a secret revolutionary club. Among the students of

St Stephen's was Har Dayal, who was in the graduating class of 1903. Though he moved to Lahore to do his M.A. and then to Oxford, he continued to be in touch with the group inside the college. Har Dayal was soon forced to go into exile in Europe, and thence to the United States of America, where he became the founder general secretary of the Ghadar Party in San Francisco.[224]

Apart from the secret activities of the club, there were frequent public meetings and attempts at wider organization. The city was sitting up and taking notice of what was happening in the rest of the country. The arrest of the nationalist leader Lala Lajpat Rai in 1907 was marked by a public meeting of protest and fund-collection drives for his anticipated trial. His arrival in the city in 1908, after his release, was greeted with a large crowd. Revolutionary activity in other parts of the country also evoked a response in the city. Funds were collected for the defence of Aurobindo Ghosh and Khudi Ram Bose in the Alipore bomb case. The city was flooded with pamphlets extolling Prafulla Chakie and Khudi Ram Bose as heroes of the cause of nationalism. When prohibitory orders against public gatherings were promulgated by the local authorities, Haidar Raza took the innovative step of shifting the meetings from Queens Garden to the eastern bank of the Yamuna, which was part of Meerut District.[225]

The authorities soon found an excuse to swoop down on Syed Haidar Raza. He had started the newspaper *Aftab*, for which he was persecuted and fined under Section 3 of the repressive Newspapers (Incitement of Offences) Act of 1908.

Further persecution prompted him to leave Delhi for a while, and finally leave India in 1909. The vacuum was filled by Amir Chand who, in 1908, had resigned from the St Stephen's School and now ran a newspaper, *Akash*. One of his activities was the translation of nationalist writings from the rest of the country into Urdu, and their distribution as pamphlets.[226]

For various reasons, however, by then the Swadeshi movement had lost steam, even on an all-India level. In Delhi, one of the causes was internal dissension. The first decade of the century saw some communal tension, particularly due to the aggressive Shuddhi campaign of the Arya Samaj, aimed at converting Muslims and other Hindus to the fold. These tensions were expressed through the press, pamphleteering and public meetings, and the Sanatan Hindus were also motivated to form organizations to counter the Samaj. The Councils Act of 1909 (popularly called the Morley-Minto Reforms) increased the number of elected members in the Imperial and provincial legislative councils, but introduced the insidious principle of separate electorates. This issue of separate electorates—by which Muslim voters could only vote for Muslim candidates in constituencies reserved for them, caused a Hindu-Muslim rift and took the edge off nationalist politics. The British found an opportunity to crack down using the draconian Press Act of 1910, and the national movement, under Amir Chand, was forced to go underground.[227]

On another front, Delhi once again became the venue for a Coronation Durbar. George V, who succeeded to his father's throne in 1910, was the first British monarch to visit

India for the Durbar, and was to be the last. The scale of the gathering was unprecedented, with 250,000 people arriving in Delhi. This time around, an even greater attempt was made to invoke memories of the heyday of the Mughal empire and symbolically merge them with the images of the new emperor. So, instead of arriving at the main railway station in the city, the emperor and his consort alighted at a small station in Salimgarh, which was just north of, and internally connected to, the Red Fort. This was done 'so that he could issue forth before his people from the gates of the old Imperial fortress, and thus revive an ancient memory'. A similar effect was sought to be achieved by the darshan, akin to the practice that had been followed by the Mughals. The royal couple sat on thrones on the terrace of the fort near the Jharokha, so that the people could see them from the banks of the Yamuna below. The darshan was cleverly arranged to coincide with a mela that had been organized on the sands below the fort. This automatically provided a throng as an audience.[228]

Held in the backdrop of nationalist activity, the Durbar of 1911 involved a great number of security measures and a huge presence of troops. The Delhi Durbar Police Act (1911) was promulgated, and listed thirty-three activities that were prohibited. These ranged from begging or loitering, to trespassing within any of the Durbar camps or on parade grounds, and damaging or defacing public property. A highly ambiguous item on the list was punishment threatened to anyone who 'loiters, lurks, or is found in any place under such circumstances as to raise a suspicion that he was about to commit, or aid in the commission of, an offence, or that he was waiting for an opportunity to commit an offence'. These legal measures were accompanied by the precautionary arrest of 300 'dangerous characters'.[229]

A large crowd turned out to see the procession, though, again, the people were largely silent. The popular explanation given this time was that George V, who had chosen to ride a horse rather than an elephant, had initially not been recognized. The truth was that most Indians probably recognized the futility of this extravagant pageantry, and the attempt to revive outdated conventions in a complete misreading of the political mood. Nevertheless, the people of Shahjahanabad were always up for a fair, and many must no doubt have attended the mela below the fort.[230]

The remote Durbar site was, as before, largely inaccessible to most of the citizens of Delhi, but here there occurred a development that was to have a long-term impact on Shahjahanabad. In a speech at the very end of the Durbar proceedings on 12 December, the new emperor announced the decision to move the capital from Calcutta to Delhi. This was followed up, on the 15th, with the laying of the foundation stones of the new capital of the empire. The stones were laid in the Durbar camp itself, several miles north of Shahjahanabad, though the eventual site of the new capital would be to the south of the Mughal city. The next few decades would bring Delhi into the spotlight as it became the seat of a vast empire, but soon, with the rise of the grand new capital city, Shahjahanabad itself would be pushed into the shadows.

But meanwhile, its status as the capital brought Delhi into the focus not only of the government, but also of revolutionary nationalist activity. The group that had been active during the Swadeshi movement, had gone underground, and had become part of a larger North Indian militant nationalist movement. They executed a daring attack on the Viceroy Hardinge on 23 December1912. The occasion was a formal 'state entry'—the arrival of the viceroy and his ceremonial procession through Shahjahanabad to mark the official shift of the capital. As the procession, with Hardinge seated on an elephant, made its way down Chandni Chowk (by this time the entire stretch of road between the Red Fort and Fatehpuri Masjid was known by this name), a bomb was thrown at him. Hardinge escaped with injuries, though the mahout driving the elephant was killed.

There was public condemnation of the act by a number of people in Delhi, who also came forward to subscribe to a fund to offer a reward for information. Eventually the government decided to bear the full expense of the reward, and the fund was instead used to finance Lady Hardinge Medical College and Hospital, and towards a new building for the Municipal Library, which was also subsequently named after Hardinge (now the Hardayal Library).

Despite the offer of a generous reward, details of the conspiracy unfolded slowly, after many months of investigation. What came to be known as the Delhi Conspiracy Case revealed the involvement of a small group of Delhi revolutionaries—among whom were Amir Chand, Avadh Behari, and Balmukund, working in concert with the

Bengal revolutionaries Rash Behari Bose and Basanta Kumar Biswas. Har Dayal, then in the US, had expressed jubilation at the bomb and accepted it as the work of his group. The trial, held in Delhi from May to September 1914, led to Amir Chand, Avadh Behari and Bal Mukund being sentenced to death. They were hanged in Delhi district jail on 8 May 1915. Basanta Kumar Biswas was also found guilty, and hanged in Lahore jail. Rash Behari Bose managed to evade arrest and fled the country some time later. On 10 February 1915, the day the judgement in the case was announced, a bomb exploded in the Delhi Club, which was housed within Ludlow Castle (a palatial home built by one Dr Ludlow in the early nineteenth century), just north of the city.[231]

Revolutionary violence had received limited support in Delhi, being the work exclusively of a group of young people, mostly teachers. Mainstream nationalist activity, however, was growing quickly, particularly as Delhi's new status as the capital brought leading nationalists to it. Mahatma Gandhi visited Delhi in 1915, soon after his return from South Africa, and stayed in the house of the principal of St Stephen's College, Sushil Kumar Rudra. Rudra's house, in fact, had become the rendezvous for a number of other nationalist leaders—Rabindranath Tagore, Madan Mohan Malviya, Gopal Krishna Gokhale, Abul Kalam Azad and S.N. Banerjea. It was here that Tagore completed his English translation of the *Gitanjali*, for which he won the Nobel Prize for Literature. Other members of the staff and students of the college were also involved in the growing national movement. These included Charles

Freer Andrews, who taught there between 1904-1913, before becoming involved full-time with the nationalist movement. A prominent student was Asaf Ali, who studied law in England after his graduation from St Stephen's and then came back to start a legal career at the Delhi Bar in 1914, simultaneously with an active involvement in nationalist politics.[232]

With the arrival of the Ali brothers, Mohammad Ali and Shaukat Ali, in 1912, Delhi also became the centre of the Khilafat movement. This movement grew out of a concern of Muslims the world over, about European aggression against Turkey from 1911, and the threat it posed to the Khilafat, the Ottoman ruler's position as the temporal leader of the Islamic state. Muhammad Ali aired his views through his Urdu daily newspaper, *Hamdard,* which he started in Delhi, and also his English weekly, *Comrade*, whose headquarters he moved from Calcutta to Delhi. However, the Delhi authorities used prohibitory orders and internment of the brothers to crack down on the movement, and so its focus shifted to Lucknow in March 1916.[233]

One branch of the nationalist movement in Delhi was closely associated with the Theosophical Society. Delhi Theosophists had opened a girls' school in 1904, the Indraprastha Hindu Kanya Shikshalaya, which soon moved to premises behind Jama Masjid, which it still occupies. Its first principal, the Australian Leonora G'Meiner, was responsible for setting up a branch of the Home Rule League in 1917. The Home Rule League, which sought self-government for India, was set up in parallel by Annie Besant and Bal Gangadhar

Tilak. In Delhi, the League's president was Miss G'Meiner, and members included Asaf Ali, Dr M.A. Ansari, Pearey Lal, and Hakim Ajmal Khan. The government hit back by withdrawing recognition as well as the grant-in-aid to the school.[234]

The growth and proliferation of these several groups, animated by anti-government feeling, meant that Delhi was set to play a leading role in the next major phase of the anti-colonial struggle. One outcome was that sixty delegates from Delhi attended the 1917 Congress session in Bombay, and in 1918, both the Congress and Muslim League sessions were held in Delhi. Then, in March 1919, Mahatma Gandhi gave a call for a Satyagrah, a non-violent protest against the 'Anarchical and Revolutionary Crimes Act 1919', popularly known as the Rowlatt Act. This act, passed in the legislative council despite the opposition of every Indian member, severely curtailed civil liberties in the name of curbing terrorism.[235]

The people of Delhi joined wholeheartedly in the protest, after Mahatma Gandhi addressed a meeting on 7 March, but probably they were animated at least as much by local grievances as by national ones. According to contemporary observers, these included the cutting down of trees along Chandni Chowk after the Hardinge bomb attack, closing of city wells after the introduction of the piped water supply, the income-tax, and the high-handed activities of the police. One interesting grievance was the strict enforcement of Municipal building by-laws[236]—apparently the people of the city have long cherished their perceived right to construct as they please!

A hartal or general strike was called on 30 March. It

started off peacefully, but there were some incidents of clashes between the crowd and the police—near the railway station, near the Town Hall, and at Pipal Park (opposite the Digambar Jain Lal Mandir). A leading role in the movement was played by Swami Shraddhanand, the Arya Samaj leader, who addressed several public gatherings with moving speeches, including one at the Jama Masjid on 4 April, after the Friday prayer. There was a hartal again on the 6th. When Gandhiji, who was due to arrive on the 9th, was prevented by the authorities, this led to a one-week hartal in Delhi starting from the 10th. The problem was that it was difficult to keep the protest from turning violent, and the outbreak of violence on the 17th gave the police an excuse to invoke the Seditious Meetings Act. Mahatma Gandhi had, meanwhile, decided to suspend the movement nation-wide due to the inability to contain violence, and this led to Swami Shraddhanand's call on the 18th for an end to the hartal.[237]

The momentum of mass protest was not immediately lost however, and in mid-1920, the Non-Cooperation movement was launched—in concert between the Congress and the Khilafat Committee. There was a boycott of foreign goods, and a few strikes during 1920-22, until the movement was withdrawn at an all-India level in early 1922. With the temporary lull in nationalist activity, there was a flaring up of communal tension. There were communal riots in 1924, in response to which Gandhiji, who had only recently been released from jail, arrived in Delhi. He stayed at the house of Mohammad Ali and undertook a twenty-one day fast in the cause of Hindu-Muslim unity. The resulting peace was only temporary, as riots recurred over the next three years, the nadir being reached with the assassination of Swami Shraddhanand in December 1926.[238]

The pattern that was repeated through the period of national struggle was one of alternating periods of anti-colonial activity and communal tension. When the anti-colonial struggle was strong, people would forget their communal grievances and join hands. Whenever, and for whatever reason, the anti-colonial movement slackened, communalism would rear its ugly head again. In fact, often it was the same people who would agitate for national causes, and then for communal ones.

The political developments of the 1910s and 1920s were taking place against the backdrop of some important changes in the relationship of Shahjahanabad with its immediate surroundings. As soon as the transfer of the capital from Calcutta had been announced, planning had begun to construct a grand new city. Work began on New Delhi, for which a location south of Shahjahanabad was ultimately chosen. But since this was inevitably going to take some time, the temporary capital was to be housed in Civil Lines from December 1912. This was the area outside the northern wall of Shahjahanabad, where the bulk of the British population had started living, particularly after the revolt of 1857, in preference to within the walls of the city. The European Club, which was initially housed in the Town Hall, had moved in 1898 into Ludlow Castle, in Civil Lines. In 1908, the Cantonment had moved from Daryaganj to the Ridge, and the offices of the Commissioner and Deputy Commissioner from Kashmiri Gate to Civil Lines.[239]

The transfer of the capital necessitated the provision of considerable accommodation. A new Secretariat was built (and today houses the Delhi Legislative Assembly), and Thomas Metcalfe's palatial house was repaired (it today houses the Defence Research and Development Organization). The Viceroy was housed in a refurbished circuit house. There was also a demand for more hotels. The Maidens Hotel had been built in 1900, and the Cecil and Swiss hotels were added to this area in the 1920s.

Both these spaces—Civil Lines and New Delhi—developed as essentially European enclaves. Not only did Shahjahanabad not receive anywhere close to the funding and attention that civic amenities in the European areas did, the needs of the latter began to act as a brake on the improvement of the old city. In the words of a special officer appointed in 1935 to look into the problem of congestion, after 1911 'Town planning of the older city received attention mainly in its relation to the requirements of the New Capital'. The more Shahjahanabad was neglected, the more it was reduced to the status of an 'Indian town', increasingly looked at as posing a threat to the European areas—through its congestion and resulting unsanitary conditions, as well as by its political volatility.[240]

This perception of Shahjahanabad as a threat resulted in elaborate police measures to insulate passing dignitaries, including high officials such as the Viceroy. In 1921, the

Metcalfe House, repaired in preparation for the transfer of the capital.

Duke of Connaught, the uncle of George V, visited Delhi. His route from the station to the Viceregal lodge (now the Vice Chancellor's office in Delhi University North Campus) was lined with troops facing the road and police facing the crowd, with the crowd being kept at least 12-15 yards from the carriage in which he travelled. Barriers were erected at Kashmiri Gate and Chandni Chowk to hold back the crowds.[241]

Sandwiched, as it was, between these settlements to the north and south, with the river to the east, there was little room for the expansion of Shahjahanabad. On the other hand, the population of the city had been growing at a rapid rate, driven by commercial growth, which, by the early twentieth century, had made Delhi effectively the commercial capital of North India. The only space available was to the west of Shahjahanabad. Part of the requirement for commercial space was met by dismantling the city wall along the western perimeter, and creating Burn Bastion Road (more popularly called Naya Bazar) and Garstin Bastion Road (now officially Swami Shraddhanand Marg but still often called GB Road). Then, a larger suburb to the west, which included Karol Bagh, was developed in a planned manner, and christened 'Western Extension Area'. Even this expansion did little to alleviate the congestion within the walls. In view of the better civic conditions in Civil Lines, an increasing number of wealthy Indians began to build houses and live there from the 1920s onwards.[242]

The Delhi Improvement Trust, which came into being in

1937, focused on the problems of Shahjahanabad, but again with a view to improving aesthetics and sanitation in relation to New Delhi, or making it financially remunerative. One of the first projects was housing and street development in Daryaganj, which had been lying desolate and shabby after the removal of the cantonment in 1908. Here an important consideration was that the area lay 'on the side of one of the main thoroughfares between Delhi and New Delhi.' Similarly, the vast ground that had been left vacant around the Red Fort after the post-Revolt demolitions, was irrigated and landscaped, as it presented 'a drear spectacle of dusty untidiness in the heart of India's capital'. Paharganj received attention in sanitation and aesthetics, mainly because it lay between Shahjahanabad and the new capital, and adjoined the New Delhi railway station.[243]

The administration's perception of Shahjahanabad as a dangerous, unhealthy space, which had to be kept separate from New Delhi, is best illustrated by the controversy over the city wall on the southern side. In the plan of the new city, a wide strip of land had been left vacant as a cordon sanitaire between the limits of New Delhi and the wall of Shahjahanabad. Proposals to dismantle the wall in order to free up more space, or even due to concerns of safety, since the wall was damaged in parts, were vigorously resisted by the New Delhi Municipal Committee (NDMC, a precursor to the present New Delhi Municipal Council) which had been set up in 1927. The President of the NDMC saw the population of Shahjahanabad and their problems as a contagion that had to be kept hidden from view and contact with the new capital. He went on to say, 'If ever Government decided to demolish the wall, the NDMC would insist on an absolute unclimbable fence being erected in its place, and erected before the wall was demolished'. It was suggested by officials that the wall was needed to provide a picturesque backdrop to the park that had been constructed to the south of it, as well as 'hide the horrors which doubtless exist behind it'.[244]

When the need to demolish the wall was finally accepted, it was with the condition that a row of buildings with aesthetic facades should face the road, and that the 'slums' within be cleared and redeveloped. The latter however led to protests from residents, who insisted on their right to live in their ancestral homes as they always had, and led to the project being indefinitely postponed.[245]

The collapse of the Non-Cooperation movement and a phase of quietude in the Congress led to the channelling of nationalist sentiments in another direction. A group of young men, influenced by socialist ideas, were organizing themselves to use mass struggle to overthrow the colonial state. They met at the Feroze Shah Kotla ground in September 1928, to form the Hindustan Socialist Republican Association (or Army), under the leadership of Chandrashekhar Azad and Bhagat Singh. Soon after, the movement took a violent turn. The precipitating factor was the death of Lala Lajpat Rai from injuries inflicted by police lathis during a demonstration in Lahore. In retaliation, Saunders, the police officer responsible for the lathi charge, was assassinated in Lahore, and a bomb was thrown in the Legislative Assembly in Delhi, on 8 April 1929.[246]

The bomb, thrown by B.K. Dutt and Bhagat Singh, had been quite harmless, and the idea had been to attract attention. To this end revolutionary leaflets had been thrown as well. The two gave themselves up readily, and used the subsequent trial and imprisonment for anti-government propaganda. They adopted defiant attitudes in the courtroom, and shouted revolutionary slogans. This gained them immense sympathy, not only in Delhi, but all across the nation.[247]

One secret base of the revolutionaries in Delhi had been Hindu College. Nand Kishore Nigam, a young man who had been an alumnus and was then a hostel warden as well as a lecturer, had given shelter to Chandrashekhar Azad in the hostel. He subsequently had to flee when the details of the plot became known to the police. Colleges were seen by the leaders of the national movement as an important support base. Gandhiji visited Hindu College in 1930, as did many other leaders who came to address the students over the years.[248]

The year 1930 saw an intensification of the national movement during the phase of Civil Disobedience. The Dandi march by Mahatma Gandhi in Gujarat to violate the unjust salt law inspired public meetings and processions in Delhi. The arrest of Gandhiji on 5 May 1930 led to an escalation of the protests, and to police firing on a crowd in front of Gurudwara Sisganj the next day. The police also set up an armoured car patrol through important streets to maintain order. An important feature of the protests of the 1930s was the participation of women on a significant scale. The government hit back at the movement by declaring the Congress illegal, arresting leaders, confiscating property, suppressing the press and taking strong action against non-payment of taxes.[249] In the midst of that atmosphere of political unrest, the inauguration of New Delhi took place, in February 1931. A part of the celebrations was a mela, open to the public, held in front of the Red Fort, the day after the inauguration. The events included wrestling matches, equestrian displays by cavalry regiments, fireworks and an aerial performance by the Royal Air Force.[250]

Civil Disobedience was withdrawn in 1932, and there was a lull in the national movement for a while. Communal eruptions however succeeded in keeping the atmosphere in the city tense over the next several years, with acrimonious situations developing particularly during religious festivals and observances.[251]

Small acts of defiance against the state continued, sometimes from unexpected quarters. The young students of the Indraprastha Girls School, who were part of the Girl Guides movement, in 1934, refused to salute the Union Jack, and to sing the British national anthem. In 1924, the Indraprastha College had also opened, and its students rapidly grew in national consciousness. Women from the college joined other students, particularly from Hindu College and Ramjas College (the latter had been founded in 1917), and participated in protest marches and meetings in the next phase of the nationalist struggle, the Quit India movement. The tikona (triangular) park outside Hindu College near Kashmiri Gate became a focus for public meetings and demonstrations.[252]

The Quit India movement was formally launched on 8 August 1942, with Gandhiji issuing a call for a fullscale defiance against the state, and demanding immediate and complete freedom for the nation. The government responded by immediately arresting nationalist leaders, which led to an outbreak of public protests. The Delhi Congress workers were active from the very beginning of the Quit India movement. There was a large-scale distribution of pamphlets and participation in demonstrations and picketing. Prominent leaders in the city included Aruna Asaf Ali, Desh Bandhu Gupta, Jugal Kishore Khanna, Saytavati (granddaughter of Swami Shraddhanand) and Premjas Rai. Many of them had to operate underground for years, constantly under threat of imminent arrest. The movement also involved acts of violence, such as the attempt to set fire to the Chandni Chowk post office.[253]

The authorities responded by a conspicuous deployment of the police and the army, which did not hesitate to open fire on numerous occasions. Harsh measures throughout the country were justified on the grounds that World War II was on, and no compromise could be made on the security of the state. An important priority of the armed forces was the protection of British officials. To this end, armed convoys were deputed to escort British officials living in Civil Lines, to their offices in New Delhi, since they would be passing through the potentially dangerous space of Shahjahanabad.[254]

The end of the war brought with it the release of imprisoned nationalist leaders, and also the INA trials. Subhash Chandra Bose's Indian National Army, composed of Indian prisoners of war, had accompanied the Japanese army to the Indo-Burma front. Their intention was to overthrow British rule by the force of arms. With the retreat of the Japanese, many members of the INA had been captured and brought back, and their leaders arraigned for trial. The trials, held in the Red Fort, saw prominent Congress leaders such as Jawaharlal Nehru, Asaf Ali, Tej Bahadur Sapru, Bhulabhai Desai, and K.N. Katju appearing to defend the prisoners. The trial attracted great attention, not only in Delhi, but all over the country, and provided an issue around which diverse groups could rally.[255]

The protests in support of the INA prisoners were a part of the last upswell of mass opinion against British rule. The writing was clearly on the wall, and the government could see it. By early 1946, the reality of Independence had been accepted, and the details were worked out in the following months. 1947 brought with it independence for the nation, but it also brought Partition. The country was to be divided between two nations—India and Pakistan.

The formal ceremonies marking Independence were held in New Delhi on 15 August. The next day, Jawaharlal Nehru, independent India's first prime minister, hoisted the national flag on the ramparts of the Red Fort. A crowd of some 400,000 turned up to witness the event. In the evening, there was a reception in Queen's Garden, given by the president of the Municipal Committee in honour of the prime minister and his colleagues. The streets of Shahjahanabad were illuminated and thronged with crowds.[256]

Hardly were the celebrations over than the impact of Partition began to be felt in the city. A vast migration of populations had begun and the one that would directly affect Delhi was that on the western border. Over five million would eventually cross the border in either direction. Refugees had started arriving in the city, and on 24 and 25 August, trouble was caused by some refugees forcibly occupying vacant houses. This was followed up by attacks on trains in which Muslims were leaving. This necessitated the imposition of curfew from the evening of the 28th. According to reports, the cause of the trouble was acts of aggression by the incoming refugees. The situation continued to deteriorate. There was rioting which resulted in firing by the police and military firing on 4 and 5 September. A bomb exploded in Fatehpuri mosque on the 5th. Shoot at sight orders were followed by heavy firing.[257]

Patrolling by the military brought things under some degree of control by 11 September.[258] In the meanwhile, the administration was taking various measures to bring the situation under control and to help victims. Muslims began to be moved into camps for their safety, notably into a camp set up within Purana Qila. A Delhi Emergency Committee was established, and headquartered in the Town Hall. Its meetings were attended by Pandit Nehru, who also toured Delhi and its surroundings, talking to people about the need to maintain peace. Sardar Vallabhbhai Patel induced Sikh leaders to issue an appeal on 10 September to members of their community to cooperate in maintaining peace. An important role was also played by Gandhiji, who arrived in Delhi soon after the outbreak of violence. He visited refugee camps and held prayer meetings, though one prayer meeting was disrupted by protests against recitations from the Koran.[259]

Over the next days and weeks, sporadic violence continued in Shahjahanabad. The local administration made a somewhat ham-handed effort to promote peace through the use of propaganda vans which went around the city with loud hailers, proclaiming—'Muslims, Sikhs, Hindus, be friends, be one'. Not surprisingly, they were greeted with hostility. Maulana Azad and Gandhiji made great efforts to talk to people, praying to Hindus and Sikhs to maintain peace and persuading Muslims to stay. The interesting phenomenon was that most Muslims insisted that their neighbours of other faiths, with whom they had lived in harmony for so long, were not the source of hostility. They, in fact, often protected them against aggression by incoming refugees.[260]

By October, things were largely quiet, but many Muslims had left. In early October some 120,000 Muslims were in camps all around Delhi. This number fell sharply by the end of that month as increasing numbers left for Pakistan. Starting in late September, a few thousand were induced to gradually return to their homes, despite occasional violence and cases where attempts were made to occupy their houses by force. One major reason to return was the terrible condition in the refugee camps, which had poor sanitation and outbreaks of cholera.[261]

The camps for Muslims fleeing violence or waiting to

depart were outside Shahjahanabad. There were camps for incoming refugees as well, and two of these were in Shahjahanabad. One was opposite the Delhi Main Station, and one was at an Arya Samaj institution, Diwan Hall, opposite the Red Fort. The Delhi Central Refugee Relief Committee was constituted, and it managed these camps quite efficiently, funded mostly by public contributions. Measures were taken against cholera outbreaks through inoculation camps organized at the Town Hall.[262]

The influx of displaced people into Delhi would continue for some years after independence. The refugees who poured in would eventually outnumber by far those who had left. In Shahjahanabad, the newcomers generally occupied houses vacated by those who had departed, not adding any significant newer residential units. It was New Delhi and its surroundings that saw the start of what would become the sprawl of the metropolitan area. Within Shahjahanabad, such new construction as there was, consisted of commercial units—shops and stalls, constructed to provide a livelihood to the displaced people. This included shops in some of the areas that had been left vacant after the post-1857 demolitions, such as Lajpat Rai Market and Esplanade Road. Shops were also built on Garstin Bastion Road, in Daryaganj, and adjoining the gardens north of Chandni Chowk.[263]

As had happened in 1857, the upheaval of 1947 led to a major change in the population of the old city. Large numbers of people left, and were replaced by others, though they came in at a faster rate than after 1857. But Shahjahanabad absorbed them, as it had done so many in the past.

The Jama Masjid today, and what was once the Khas Bazaar.

Shahjahanabad Today

I ENJOY VISITING SHAHJAHANABAD, AND FREQUENTLY GO THERE. The Delhi Metro, today efficiently transports numerous tourists, shoppers and others who want to experience the many attractions of 'Old Delhi', into the heart of the city. This neighbourhood of Delhi, which many simply call Chandni Chowk, means different things to different people. I see in it centuries of history, as well as a vibrant contemporary culture.

The history lies in its many landmarks. The Red Fort is a well-kept monument, a UNESCO World Heritage Site. The story of the tribulations, as well as the good times it has seen, is evident in its beautiful Mughal buildings, and equally in the mid-nineteenth century barracks beside them. The Yamuna river, which once flowed close beneath its eastern wall, has, long ago, changed its course. Now, when I look down from the terrace, close to where the emperor gave darshan to his subjects, I see, not the sandy bank he saw, but the Ring Road. The incessant buzz of traffic has replaced the elephant fights and melas that were once held here. The stream of water that once passed through the gardens and buildings of the palace complex has dried up, too.

There is a faded elegance in the beautiful courts and palaces where the Mughal emperors and their extended families once lived and worked. Most of the buildings in the complex were destroyed after the Revolt of 1857. Within the few that survived, many of the inlaid semi-precious stones and the gilding, have long ago been removed by plunderers. Yet, these structures are a testament to the high point of Mughal architecture, and throng with visitors, who come from all corners of the globe, to marvel at them.

The Red Fort does not communicate directly with the city, as it once did, through its great portals, the Lahore and Delhi Gates. Both are now surrounded by barbicans, built by Aurangzeb, who enjoyed an uneasy relationship with the people of Delhi, after his usurpation of the throne. The high red walls of the complex, however, still dominate the city that spreads out around it.

The street in front of the Lahore Gate of the Red Fort is usually busy, even chaotic. The traffic, a bewildering variety of motorized and other vehicles, the crowds, and the buzz, can be overwhelming. The details may have changed, but to me, the spirit is not very different from the time when this was the Urdu bazaar and the bustling Chowk Sa'adullah Khan. No royal elephants go down the Chandni Chowk street, but it is frequently used for colourful religious and other processions. The religious processions are numerous and varied, because this is a neighbourhood that retains the religious diversity that characterized it during Mughal rule. On this one street which stretches westwards from the Fort, you can find Jain and Hindu temples, two mosques, a gurudwara and a church.

At the head of the street, the Jain Lal Mandir has stood since

The busy road in front of the Lahore Gate of the Red Fort, showing the Jain Lal Mandir.

the time of Shahjahan, and its attached charity bird hospital is well known throughout Delhi. Not far from it lies Dariba Kalan and the mohalla Dharampura adjoining it, dominated by the Jain business class, as in Shahjahan's time. People come from all over Delhi to shop for jewellery in Dariba, and to indulge in jalebis from the 'Old and Famous Jalebiwala'. Off Dariba lies Kinari Bazaar, full of the glitter of gilt laces, sequins, and, these days, Swarovski elements. Home dressmakers as well as professional dress designers come here to source these accessories for their creations. No wedding is complete without a trip to Kinari Bazar for some bling.

Dariba Kalan and Kinari Bazar are only two of several specialist markets in Shahjahanabad. Khari Baoli, close to the Fatehpuri Masjid, is known for its spices, nuts and dried fruits. It is also dense with some iconic eateries, including the original outlet of Giani ice cream, and Chaina Ram, the famous sweet shop. Katra Neel, named after the indigo that was once used here to dye fabrics, now trades in fabrics and readymade clothes generally. Behind the Jama Masjid is Chawri Bazar, where dealers in hardware and paper ply their trade. Once this was where courtesans lived, but the advent of a more puritanical age has led to them being shifted out.

Some old landmarks of Mughal Shahjahanabad have disappeared. The Kotwali Chowk is no longer known by that name, because the police station that once gave it the name was pulled down in the last century, to make way for the expansion of the Gurudwara Sisganj. This gurudwara was built in the late eighteenth century to commemorate the place where Guru Tegh Bahadur was executed in 1675. The Sunehri Masjid, where Nadir Shah sat and oversaw the massacre of Delhi's citizens in 1739, however, still stands in this square. A new landmark, a fountain, was added after the Revolt of 1857, and since then, the chowk has popularly been known as the Phawwara, or Fountain Chowk.

Chandni Chowk, the square that has given the most important street of Shahjahanabad its name, was transformed profoundly after the Revolt of 1857. But the Clock Tower that the British subsequently built in the centre of the square, has also disappeared, having collapsed in 1951. The Town Hall building no longer houses the Municipal offices, which have moved to a new building, Delhi's tallest, outside the limits of Shahjahanabad. The chowk is still full of bustle, though. People feed pigeons in front of the Town Hall, leading to huge flocks of these birds gathering here. The pavement in front of the building is also a resting place for workmen, especially house-painters, who sit there with their simple tools, waiting to be engaged by customers. Not far from here is the haveli of Chunna Mal, built in the 1860s by that rich merchant, still dominating the street with its wide frontage.

One major landmark that has survived is the Jama Masjid. Its lofty position and impressive portals dominate the area around, and a bird's eye view of Shahjahanabad can be had from the dizzying height of its southern tower, which is open to visitors. Its vast courtyard and the long and broad flights of steps on three sides can accommodate hundreds of worshippers for congregational prayers. The Khas Bazar, which linked the mosque to the Red Fort, was destroyed in the aftermath of the Revolt. What has taken its place is a more or less informal gathering of hawkers. At the foot of the mosque is the shrine of Sarmad, the Armenian mystic friend of Dara Shukoh.

No trip to Old Delhi is complete without a taste of its street food. I particularly look forward to winters, when a special treat is sold by hawkers at street corners. This is daulat ki chaat—a light-as-air dessert of milk, sugar, nuts and saffron. I also like the nankhatai—delicate biscuits, that are freshly baked by hawkers on simple cast-iron skillets carried on carts. More permanent establishments include the standing-room-only Natraj, the purveyor of sublime chaat—particularly dahi bhalla. Many visitors also like to go to a famous culinary destination—the Parathe Wali Gali. The string of small restaurants on this street specialize in parathas—deep-fried flat breads stuffed with an amazing array of savoury and sweet fillings. Probably the oldest restaurant in Old Delhi is Karim's, west of Jama Masjid. Though it was established only slightly over a hundred years ago, its cuisine harks back to the glory days of the Mughal emperors. Run by the descendants of a cook at the royal kitchens, it serves up food that people from all over Delhi come to savour.

Food is an integral part of the culture that gives Old Delhi its distinctive identity. This culture, itself, is a product of centuries of development, and intermingling is an integral part of it. When it was founded as an imperial project in the seventeenth century, merchants, artists, artisans as well as the nobility and bureaucracy, had flocked to it from far and wide.

The Kinari Bazaar today.

Subsequent migrations have continued, some steady and some in waves, as in 1947. All those who have come to the city have enriched it with their diverse ethnic, linguistic, religious and culinary traditions, producing the 'typical' culture of the place.

The character of Shahjahanabad has changed over the decades. Its commercial role has survived and even grown, while residents have steadily moved out. Many of them continue to do business there, even while they have moved on to live in newly developed areas in other parts of Delhi. Some havelis lie locked up, others have been transformed into tenements with multiple tenants. Haphazard additions have been made, and the original two-storey havelis often now have two or three additional floors on top of them. It is only the strength of the old thin lakhori bricks, of which they are made, that keeps them up. The infrastructure is crumbling, after decades of neglect of civic amenities. Pavements are broken, drainage is faulty, and electrical wires hang overhead, posing a fire hazard.

Yet, there are pleasant residential streets, such as Churiwalan and Kucha Pati Ram, where people live, as their ancestors have for generations, in havelis with stunning carved doorways and overhanging balconies. The streets may be narrow, but there are open spaces. These are to be found, not only in the inner haveli courtyards, but on the roof-top terraces, which are places to live and work, and socialize with neighbours. Neighbourliness is built into the havelis themselves. The entrances to most havelis are flanked by otlas—stone seats, where people can sit and chat—very much like a stoop or porch.

Many of those who still continue to live here, do so because they value their ties with the city, its distinctive culture and the way of life Shahjahanabad represents. There is the neighbourliness of course, and also the convenience of living within walking distance of almost everything one might need. These factors compensate for the inconveniences, such as not having space to park a car. It is also a safe place. Without the daytime impersonality and empty darkness after hours, which characterize modern business districts, one feels safe here. Streets here are not simply conduits for traffic, they are inhabited public spaces.

Maybe it is because residents recognize how precious this way of life is, that any attempts at redevelopment of the old residential areas have been strongly resisted. The street pattern of Shahjahanabad has remained largely unchanged for the last three and a half centuries. This is not to say that the city has become a museum. It is a lively and busy place, one that is also continuously changing and adapting. The city has absorbed incoming populations across centuries, but it has also imbued them with some of its own character. The narrow lanes of Shahjahanabad, its courtyard houses and rooftop terraces, foster a certain culture—one that thrives on close contact between neighbours.

Chandni Chowk has always seen visitors coming to pray in its many places of worship, to shop in its specialist markets, to eat its famous street food, or even to visit prominent landmarks such as the Red Fort and Jama Masjid. More recently, the other attractions of Shahjahanabad are being recognized—the history that still lives in its narrow streets, and the way of life that is represented by its courtyard homes. One result of this is the recognition of the tourist potential—through the conversion of some restored havelis to heritage hotels. The other, more important sign of change is the desire of some homeowners to restore their havelis and live in them, in preference to moving out of Old Delhi altogether. Some steps are being taken to rejuvenate the infrastructure, such as the laying of underground electric cables, and the repair of streets and pavements. There are also plans to improve the surroundings of Jama Masjid.

With some amount of sensitive intervention, this historic precinct of Delhi can become an attractive place to live in, and not merely an interesting place to visit. It is only when the living conditions of residents are improved that the place will realize its full potential. The key to improvement lies within the historic forms and structures of Shahjahanabad. The havelis that have stood the test of time only need some extra help to last well into the future. Shahjahanabad has had a glorious past. I believe it has an exciting future as well.

Notes

1. W.E. Begley and Z.A. Desai, eds., *The Shah Jahan Nama of Inayat Khan*, translated by A.R. Fuller, Oxford University Press, Delhi 1990, p 570.
2. W.E. Begley and Z.A. Desai, *Taj Mahal, the Illumined Tomb*, University of Washington Press, Seattle 1989, pp 75, 266
3. Samsam ud Daulah Shahnawaz Khan and Abdul Hayy, *Maathir ul Umara*, (translated by H. Beveridge and revised by Baini Prashad), Janaki Prakashan, Patna 1979, vol 2 pp 265-66.
4. Quoted in Stephen P. Blake, *Shahjahanabad: The Sovereign City in Mughal India 1639-1739*, Cambridge University Press, New Delhi 1993, p 27.
5. *The Padma Purana, Part IX*, Motilal Banarsidass Publishers, Delhi 1956, pp 3011-15
6. Begley and Desai, *Shah Jahan Nama*, pp 406-07
7. Begley and Desai, *Taj Mahal*, pp 261-62
8. Begley and Desai, *Taj Mahal*, pp 282
9. Begley and Desai, *Taj Mahal*, p xlviii
10. Begley and Desai, *Shah Jahan Nama*, pp 403-04
11. Ebba Koch, *Mughal Architecture*, Oxford University Press, New Delhi 2002, pp 109-114.
12. For a detailed description of the buildings of the fort, see Syed Ali Nadeem Rezavi, ''The mighty defensive fort': Red Fort at Delhi under Shah Jahan—Its plan and structures as described by Muhammad Waris', *Proceedings of the Indian History Congress, 71st Session, 2010-11.*
13. Begley and Desai, *Shah Jahan Nama*, pp 406-07
14. Khan, *Maathir ul Umara*, vol 2 p 270.
15. Begley and Desai, *Shah Jahan Nama*, pp 406-09

16. Annemarie Schimmel, *The Empire of the Great Mughals: History, Art and Culture*, Oxford University Press, New Delhi 2005, p 199.
17. Begley and Desai, *Shah Jahan Nama*, p 537.
18. Francois Bernier, *Travels in the Mogul Empire, A.D. 1656-1668*, Archibald Constable, London 1891, p 242.
19. Begley and Desai, *Shah Jahan Nama*, pp 71, 318.
20. Shama Mitra Chenoy, *Shahjahanabad: A City of Delhi 1638-1857*, Munshiram Manoharlal, New Delhi 1998, p 45.
21. Khan, *Maathir ul Umara*, vol. 2 pp 273, 637-44.
22. Begley and Desai, *Taj Mahal*, pp xli, xlvi.
23. Begley and Desai, *Shah Jahan Nama*, p 530-31
24. Begley and Desai, *Shah Jahan Nama*, p 451
25. Begley and Desai, *Shah Jahan Nama*, pp 333, 452
26. Blake, *Shahjahanabad*, pp 76-81.
27. Bernier, *Travels*, pp 245-48
28. Jyotiprasad Jain, *Pramukh aitihasik Jain purush aur mahilayen*, Bhartiya Gyanpith, pp 373, 305.
29. These are some of the models that have been developed to understand the city. See Eckart Ehlers and Thomas Krafft, 'Islamic Cities in India?' in Eckart Ehlers and Thomas Krafft eds *Shahjahanabad/Old Delhi: Tradition and Colonial Change*, New Delhi 2003; Blake, *Shahjahanabad*; and Chenoy, *Shahjahanabad*.
30. Ebba Koch, *Shah Jahan and Orpheus, The Pietre Dure Decoration and the Programme of the Throne in the Hall of Public Audiences at the Red Fort of Delhi*, Akademische Druck- u. Verlagsanstalt, Graz, 1988.
31. Shireen Moosvi, *People, Taxation and Trade in Mughal India*, Oxford University Press, New Delhi 2008, p 131.
32. Begley and Desai, *Shah Jahan Nama*, pp 413, 445, 453, 476, 490, 494, 501, 505, 535, 541.
33. Bernier, *Travels*, p 260.

34. Begley and Desai, *Shah Jahan Nama*, p 567; Khafi Khan, *Muntakhab ul Lubab*, in H.M. Elliot and John Dowson, *The History of India, as told by its own historians: The Muhammadan Period*, Trubner Company, London 1867-77, vol VII, p 284
35. Begley and Desai, *Shah Jahan Nama*, pp 530, 510
36. Begley and Desai, *Shah Jahan Nama*, pp 567, 497.
37. Nicolao Manucci, *Storia do Mogor or Mogul India 1653-1708*, translated by William Irvine, John Murray, London 1907, vol 1 pp 88-90.
38. Begley and Desai, *Shah Jahan Nama*, pp 446-47
39. Begley and Desai, *Shah Jahan Nama*, p 495
40. Begley and Desai, *Shah Jahan Nama*, p 450
41. Manucci, *Storia*, vol 1 pp 94-96, 319.
42. Saqi Musta'd Khan's, *Maa'asir e Alamgiri*, translated by Jadunath Sarkar, Royal Asiatic Society of Bengal, Calcutta 1947, p 293; Jadunath Sarkar (ed), William Irvine, *Later Mughals*, Munshiram Manoharlal Publishers, New Delhi 1996, vol 1, pp 272-75.
43. Manucci, *Storia*, vol 1 pp 192-97, 218; Bernier, *Travels* pp 12-14.
44. Manucci, *Storia*, vol 1 p 195; Schimmel, *Empire of the Great Mughals*, p 158.
45. Manucci, *Storia*, vol 2 pp 35, 42
46. Manucci, *Storia*, vol 1 p 221
47. Bernier, *Travels*, pp 118, 249
48. Bernier, *Travels*, pp 243-44
49. Manucci, *Storia*, vol 1 pp 196
50. Bernier, *Travels*, pp 7, 101; Manucci, *Storia*, vol 1 p 223-24, vol 2 p 154
51. S.M. Ikram, *Muslim Civilization in India*, Columbia University Press, New York 1964, p 187-88
52. Manucci, *Storia*, vol 1 p 241-42
53. Begley and Desai, *Shah Jahan Nama*, p 543
54. Begley and Desai, *Shah Jahan Nama*, pp 551-56, 563-65

55. Begley and Desai, *Shah Jahan Nama*, pp 554-63
56. Begley and Desai, *Shah Jahan Nama*, p 559
57. Khan, *Muntakhab ul Lubab*, vol VII, pp 245-46.
58. Khan, *Muntakhab ul Lubab*, p 246; Begley and Desai, *Shah Jahan Nama*, p 560
59. Saida Dehlvi, *The Sufi Courtyard: Dargahs of Delhi*, Harper Collins India, Noida 2012, p 207.
60. Khan, *Muntakhab ul Lubab*, pp 246-47, 263-64.
61. Manucci, *Storia do Mogor*, vol 2 pp 5-7
62. Khan, *Muntakhab ul Lubab*, pp 283-84.
63. Khan, *Maa'asir e Alamgiri*, pp 45, 48-52, 90, 100.
64. J.P. Losty and Malini Roy, *Mughal India: Art, Culture and Empire*, The British Library, London 2012, p 85; Schimmel, *Great Mughals*, pp 270,
65. Satish Chandra, 'Cultural and Political Role of Delhi, 1675-1725' in R.E. Frykenberg ed, *Delhi Through the Ages*, Oxford University Press, New Delhi 1986, pp 109; Khan, *Maa'asir e Alamgiri*, p 322.
66. J.S. Grewal and Irfan Habib eds, *Sikh History from Persian Sources*, Tulika, New Delhi 2001, pp 92, 105, 214; M.K. Pal, *Historical Gurudwaras of Delhi*, Niyogi Books, New Delhi 2013, pp 82-3; Hardip Singh Syan, *Sikh Militancy in the Seventeenth Century*, I. B. Tauris, London, New York, 2012, *passim*.
67. Khan, *Maa'asir e Alamgiri*, pp 78, 94-95.
68. Satish Chandra, 'Jizyah and the State in India during the Seventeenth Century' and 'Religious Policy of Aurangzeb during the Latter Part of his Reign' in *Essays on Medieval Indian History*, Oxford University Press, New Delhi 2003, pp 305-45.
69. Khan, *Muntakhab ul Lubab*, p 296.
70. Khan, *Maa'asir e Alamgiri*, pp 36, 126, 132.
71. Chandra, 'Cultural and Political Role of Delhi', pp 109-11.
72. Irvine, *Later Mughals*, vol 1, pp 190-97, 241
73. Irvine, *Later Mughals*, vol 1, pp 219-20, 236-55.

74. Irvine, *Later Mughals*, vol 1, pp 275-81
75. Shamsur Rahman Faruqi, *Burning Rage, Icy Scorn: The Poetry of Ja'far Zatalli,* Lecture at University of Texas, Austin, 24 September 2008, p 3.
76. Irvine, *Later Mughals*, vol 1, pp 290, 304-05
77. Irvine, *Later Mughals*, vol 1, pp 312-18
78. Irvine, *Later Mughals*, vol 1, pp 382-86
79. Irvine, *Later Mughals*, vol 1, pp 387- 395
80. Irvine, *Later Mughals*, vol 1, p 395
81. Irvine, *Later Mughals*, vol 1, pp 389, 417-18, 430-31; vol 2, pp 1-2, 56-60, 91-92
82. Khan, *Muntakhab ul Lubab*, pp 496-97
83. Irvine, *Later Mughals*, vol 2, pp, 103,
84. Khan, *Muntakhab ul Lubab*, p 485
85. Irvine, *Later Mughals*, vol 2, pp, 257-63
86. Khan and Hayy, *Maathir ul Umara*, 52, vol 2, pp 419-21. Irvine, *Later Mughals*, vol 2, pp 288-95
87. Irvine, *Later Mughals*, vol 2, pp 330-50
88. Irvine, *Later Mughals*, vol 2, p 363.
89. Irvine, *Later Mughals*, vol 2, pp 364, 375.
90. Irvine, *Later Mughals*, vol 2, pp 364-66
91. Irvine, *Later Mughals*, vol 2, pp 367-70
92. Irvine, *Later Mughals*, vol 2, pp 371-74
93. Dargah Quli Khan, *Muraqq-e-Dehli*, translated by Khaliq Anjum, Anjuman Taraqqi-e-Urdu Hind, New Delhi 1993.
94. Khan, *Muraqqa*, pp 137-38, 176
95. Khan, *Muraqqa*, pp 176-77
96. Khan, *Muraqqa*, pp 178, passim.
97. Khan, *Muraqqa*, pp 137-39, 142-43, 154, 169-71, 183.
98. Khan, *Muraqqa*, pp 160-68, 173-75.
99. Khan, *Muraqqa*, pp 122-23
100. For an excellent explanation of the world of Urdu poetry, especially the ghazal, see Pritchett, *Nets of Awareness,* pp 77-122

101. For a brief but informative account of mushairas and other institutions of Urdu poetry see Frances W. Pritchett, 'A Long History of Urdu Literary Culture, Part 2: Histories, Performances, and Masters' in Sheldon Pollock ed. *Literary Cultures in History: Reconstructions from South Asia*, New Delhi 2003, p 864 onwards, and also Pritchett, *Nets of Awareness*; and Haneef Naqvi, *Shoara-e-Urdu ke Tazkire, Nikat-ush-Shoara se Gulshan-e-Bekhhar tak*, Lucknow 1998, p 157.
102. Khan, *Muraqqa*, pp 125-27, 174-75.
103. Khan, *Muraqqa*, pp 128-29
104. Jain, *Jain purush aur mahilayen*, p 306
105. Khan, *Muraqqa*, pp 130—*passim*.
106. Khan, *Muraqqa*, p 136, 172-72
107. Khan, *Muraqqa*, pp 139-42
108. Tabir Kalam, *Religious Tradition and Culture in Eighteenth Century North India*, Primus Books, Delhi 2013, pp 23-38
109. Anon. *Tarikh e Ahmad Shah*, in Elliot and Dowson, *History of India*, vol VIII, p 112-14
110. Abdul Karim Khan, *Bayan e Waki*, Muhammad Ali Khan, *Tarikh e Muzaffari*, in Elliot and Dowson, *History of India*, vol VIII, pp 131-39, 317-20; Sarkar, *Fall of the Mughal Empire*, Orient Black Swan, New Delhi, 2015, vol 1, pp 175, 240-47
111. Sarkar, *Fall of the Mughal Empire*, vol 1, pp 172, 226-39, vol 2, pp 84-88, 118.
112. Sarkar, *Fall of the Mughal Empire*, vol 1, pp 260-61, 267-68;vol 2, pp 7-8, 94.
113. Sarkar, *Fall of the Mughal Empire*, vol 2, pp 53-76.
114. Sarkar, *Fall of the Mughal Empire*, vol 2, pp 147-56.
115. Sarkar, *Fall of the Mughal Empire*, vol 2, pp 229-30, 274-78.
116. Sarkar, *Fall of the Mughal Empire*, vol 2, pp 329-31.
117. Sarkar, *Fall of the Mughal Empire*, vol 3, pp 120, 137.
118. Sarkar, *Fall of the Mughal Empire*, vol 3, pp 178-79.

119. Sarkar, *Fall of the Mughal Empire*, vol 3, pp 235-38, 257-60.
120. Sarkar, *Fall of the Mughal Empire*, vol 3, pp 262-68.
121. Sarkar, *Fall of the Mughal Empire*, vol 3, p 279, vol 4, pp 182-88.
122. From Dr Amir Arifi, *Shahar ashob—Ek tajzia*, Saqi Book Depot, Delhi, 1994, p 96. Transcription from Urdu, mine.
123. From Khurshidul Islam and Ralph Russell, *Three Mughal Poets: Mir, Sauda, Mir Hasan*, Oxford University Press, New Delhi, 1994, p 67.
124. Islam and Russell, *Three Mughal Poets*, p 260. Transcription from Urdu, mine.
125. This and the following account is taken from Swapna Liddle, *Cultural History of Nineteenth Century Delhi*, unpublished PhD thesis, Jamia Millia Islamia, 2007.
126. Liddle, *Nineteenth Century Delhi*, pp 19-22.
127. Liddle, *Nineteenth Century Delhi*, pp 23-25.
128. Liddle, *Nineteenth Century Delhi*, pp 68-9; Munshi Faizuddin, *Bazm-e-Akhir*, Urdu Akademi, Delhi 1992, p 94-5; *Dehli Urdu Akhbar* 5.7.1840; 9.8.1840; 30.8.1840; 15.8.52
129. Liddle, *Nineteenth Century Delhi*, pp 27-30.
130. Nasir Nazir, *Lal Qile ki ek jhalak*, Urdu Akademi, Delhi 2001, pp 33-4; 44-7
131. *A Gazetteer of Delhi 1883-84*, (Reprint) Aryan Books International, New Delhi, 2010, p 207.
132. Barbara Daly Metcalf, *Islamic Revival in British India; Deoband 1860-1900*, New Delhi 2002, pp 46-52; Margrit Pernau, 'Multiple Identities and Communities; Re-contextualizing Religion', in Jamal Malik and Helmut Reifeld (eds.) *Religious Pluralism in South Asia and Europe*, New Delhi 2005, especially p 154.
133. Mukhtaruddin Ahmad, 'Mufti Sadruddin Azurda ki Kuchh Nayab o Kamyab Tahrirein' in Nazir Ahmad ed. *Tahqiqat: Intekhab Maqalat Ghalib Nama*, Ghalib Institute, New Delhi, 1997, pp

109-10; Abdurahman Parwaz Aslahi, *Mufti Sadruddin Azurdah*, Maktaba Jamia, New Delhi 1977, p 69-71; Metcalf, *Islamic Revival in British India*, pp 55-9; *Dehli Urdu Akhbar* 15.3.1840; 22.3.1840; 11.7.52; 31.10.52; 7.11.52

134. *Dehli Urdu Akhbar* 31.10.1852; Percival Spear, *Twilight of the Mughals*, Oxford University Press, New Delhi 2002, p 196
135. *Dehli Urdu Akhbar*, 15.3.1840
136. Liddle, *Nineteenth Century Delhi*, pp 66-7; Faizuddin, *Bazm e Akhir*, pp 82-4
137. Liddle, *Nineteenth Century Delhi*, pp 67, 70; Faizuddin, *Bazm-e-Akhir*, pp 83-84; *Dehli Urdu Akhbar* 11.10.1840 1.11.1840.
138. Liddle, *Nineteenth Century Delhi*, p 75.
139. Liddle, *Nineteenth Century Delhi*, pp 72-3
140. Liddle, *Nineteenth Century Delhi*, pp 117, 130.
141. Liddle, *Nineteenth Century Delhi*, 207-8; and Mirza Sangin Beg, *Sair-ul-Manazil*, edited and translated by Sharif Husain Qasimi, Ghalib Institute, New Delhi 1982, p 178.
142. Liddle, *Nineteenth Century Delhi*, pp 106, 207; Syed Ahmad Khan, *Asarussanadid*, Urdu Akademi, Delhi 2000, p 709
143. For a good biography of Skinner, see Dennis Holman, *Sikandar Sahib: James Skinner 1778-1841*, Heinemann, London 1961.
144. Qasimi trans, *Sair ul Manazil*, pp 186, 190; Liddle, *Nineteenth Century Delhi*, p 105; For the location and extent of the church as well as Skinner's mansion, see the large map of Shahjahanabad in Ehlers and Krafft eds. *Shahjahanabad/Old Delhi;* Memoir of Emily Bayley, daughter of Thomas Metcalfe, in M.M. Kaye ed. *The Golden Calm*, Webb and Bower, Exeter, 1980, pp 14-5
145. Liddle, *Nineteenth Century Delhi*, p 105
146. Khan, *Asarussanadid*, pp 518, 560-2, 582; and *Sira-e-Faridiya*, p 33; Aslahi, *Mufti Sadruddin Azurda*, p 27; Pritchett, *Nets of Awareness*, p 14; Farhatullah Beg, *Daktar Nazir Ahmad ki Kahani, Kuch Meri aur Kuchh un ki Zabani*, Anjuman Taraqqi Urdu,

Delhi 1992, p 42; Christina Osterheld, 'Deputy Nazir Ahmad and the Delhi College' in Margrit Pernau ed. *The Delhi College: Traditional Elites, the Colonial State, and Education before 1857*, New Delhi 2006, p 301
147. Liddle, *Nineteenth Century Delhi*, pp 160-61
148. Liddle, *Nineteenth Century Delhi* pp 161-62
149. Margrit Pernau, 'Preparing a Meeting-Ground: C.F. Andrews, St. Stephen's, and the Delhi College' in C.F. Andrews *Zaka Ullah of Delhi*, Oxford University Press, New Delhi, 2003, p lxv
150. Emma Roberts, *Scenes and Characteristics of Hindostan*, W.H. Allen, London, 1835, vol III, pp 167, 171, 174.
151. Abdul Haq, *Marhum Dehli Kalij*, Anjuman Taraqqi Urdu, New Delhi 1989, pp 134-55; Gail Minault, 'Delhi College and Urdu', *The Annual of Urdu Studies,* University of Wisconsin, Madison, Number 14, 1999.
152. *Dehli Urdu Akhbar* 21.11.1841, 28.6.1840, 15.8.1841, 1.2.52; 2.10.53
153. Dhruv Raina and S. Irfan Habib, *Domesticating Modern Science: A Social History of Science and Culture in Colonial India*, Tulika, New Delhi 2004; Gail Minault, 'The Perils of Cultural Mediation: Master Ram Chandra and Academic Journalism at Delhi College', in Pernau ed. *The Delhi College*, pp 194-200.
154. Maulvi Karimuddin, *Guldasta e Nazninan*, Patna 1972, pp 6-8; Karimuddin, *Tabqat Shoara e Hind*, Uttar Pradesh Urdu Akademi, Lucknow 1983, introduction, pp 400, 415, 468-9; Dr Mahmud Ilahi ed., Maulvi Karimuddin, *Khat e Taqdir*, Lucknow 1965, pp 37-39
155. Karimuddin, *Tabqat Shoara e Hind*, pp 470-71
156. *Qiran us Sadaen* n.d. 1854.
157. *Qiran us Sadaen* n.d. 1854; Khan, *Asarussanadid*, pp 149-51, 167-8
158. Karimuddin, *Tabqat Shoara e Hind*, pp 219, 329, 331, 340, 371, Qutubuddin 'Batin', *Gulistan e Bekhizan*, Uttar Pradesh Urdu

Akademi, Lucknow 1982, p 281; Abdul Ghafur 'Nasakh', *Sukhan Shoara*, Uttar Pradesh Urdu Akademi, Lucknow 1982, p 46-7; Qadir Baksh 'Sabir', *Gulistan e Sukhan*, Uttar Pradesh Urdu Akademi, Lucknow 1982, p 161-3; Mohammad Hussain Azad, *Ab e Hayat*, (translated and edited by Frances Pritchett in association with Shamsur Rahman Faruqi), Oxford University Press, New Delhi 2001, pp 375-6

159. *Dehli Urdu Akhbar* 24.10.1841; 22.8.52; 8.8.52, and *Muhibb e Hind*
160. Tanvir Ahmad Alavi, *Auraq e Ma'ani:, Ghalib ke Farsi Khutut, Urdu Tarjuma*, Urdu Akademi, Delhi 2001, p 223; Ali Jawad Zaidi, *Tarikh e Mushaira*, Shah e Hind Publications, Delhi 1992, pp 106-7
161. Said Mobarik Shah, *The City of Delhi During the Siege*, (translated by R.M. Edwards), 1859, The British Library, India Office Collection, Mss Eur B 138, pp 3-5, 30; Charles Theophilus Metcalfe, *Two Native Narratives of the Mutiny in Delhi*, Archibald Constable, Westminster 1898, pp 54, 58-9; Liddle, *Nineteenth Century Delhi*, p 249; *Dehli Urdu Akhbar*, 17 May 1857; Syed Zahiruddin Zahir Dehlavi, *Dastan-e-Ghadar*, Areeb Publications, New Delhi, 2008, p 118.
162. *Dehli Urdu Akhbar*, 17 May 1857; Haq, *Marhum Dehli Kalij*, pp 72-73; Zahir Dehlavi, *Dastan-e-Ghadar*, p 98
163. Narrative of Muinuddin Hasan Khan, in Metcalfe, *Two Native Narratives*, p 47; Zahir Dehlavi, *Dastan-e-Ghadar*, pp 97-98
164. Metcalfe, *Two Native Narratives*, p 87
165. Shah, *The City of Delhi During the Siege*, pp 7, 31.
166. Salim Qureshi and Syed Ashur Kazmi ed. and trans. *1857 ke Ghaddaron ke Khutut*, Anjuman Taraqqi Urdu, New Delhi 2001, pp 89, 93, 113, 148, 153, 95, 118, 160, 120-1, 133, 148; Metcalfe, *Two Native Narratives*, p 111; Darkhashan Tajwar ed. and trans, *Sarguzisht-e-Dehli: 1857 ke Andolan ki Kahani, Jivan Lal ki Zabani*, Rampur Raza Library, Rampur 2005, pp 191-92.

167. Liddle, *Nineteenth Century Delhi*, pp 268-69; Tajwar, *Sarguzisht-e-Dehli*, pp 82, 96, 192, 205, 214, 273, 304, 308; S.M. Azizuddin Husain, *Dastaveza-e-Ghadar 1857*, Kanishka Publishers, New Delhi 2007, p 154; *Dehli Urdu Akhbar*, 14 June 1857; Qureshi and Kazmi ed. *Ghaddaron ke Khutut*, p 146.
168. Liddle, *Nineteenth Century Delhi*, p 263
169. *Dehli Urdu Akhbar*, 21 June 1857
170. *Dehli Urdu Akhbar*, 14 June 1857
171. The official English translation of the proclamation. Liddle, *Nineteenth Century Delhi*, p 262
172. Tajwar ed. and trans, *Sarguzisht-e-Dehli*, pp 125, 127, 185-86; W. Muir, *Records of the Intelligence Department of the Government of the North Western Provinces of India During the Mutiny of 1857*, T&T Clark, Edinburgh, 1902, vol II p 38; Qureshi and Kazmi ed. *Ghaddaron ke Khutut*, p 102, 112; Husain, *Dastavezat-e-Ghadar 1857*, pp 56, 59, 67, 134; Sir Henry W. Norman and Mrs Keith Young, *Delhi 1857*, Low Price Publications, Delhi 2001, p 171; Metcalfe, *Two Native Narratives*, pp 69, 98-100; Liddle, *Nineteenth Century Delhi*, pp 258-59
173. Mirza Khan 'Dagh', in Arifi, *Shahar Ashob*, p 161, translation mine
174. Zahir Dehlavi, *Dastan-e-Ghadar*, pp 108-9, 138; Metcalfe, *Two Native Narratives*, pp 68, 102, 118; Muir, *Records of the Intelligence Department,* vol I, p 495; Tajwar, *Sarguzisht-e-Dehli*, pp 162-63; Sabri, *1857 ke Mujahid Shoara*, pp 56, 124; Norman and Young, *Delhi 1857*, p 243
175. Zahir Dehlavi, *Dastan-e-Ghadar*, p 91
176. Mohammad Zahur 'Zahur', in Arifi, *Shahar Ashob*, p 190, translation mine
177. Tajwar ed. and trans, *Sarguzisht-e-Dehli*, p 187, 199, 253, 267; Norman and Young, *Delhi 1857*, pp 91-93, 104, 119-22; Qureshi and Kazmi ed. *Ghaddaron ke Khutut*, pp 95, 118

178. Tajwar ed. and trans, *Sarguzisht-e-Dehli*, pp 232, 310; Qureshi and Kazmi ed. *Ghaddaron ke Khutut*, pp 117, 131-33, 137-38, 147-8, 153, 167, 178, 182, 188; Liddle, *Nineteenth Century Delhi*, pp 272-73; Shah, *The City of Delhi during the Siege*, p 176.
179. Muir, *Records of the Intelligence Department*, vol I p 526, vol II p 267; Liddle, *Nineteenth Century Delhi*, pp 277-79
180. Liddle, *Nineteenth Century Delhi*, pp 280-81; Raffi Gregorian, 'LOOT! The British Army and Prize Money in India, 1754-1864', senior honours thesis, University of Pennsylvania, 1986, p 39, 41, 49; Muir, *Records of the Intelligence Department*, vol II p 288
181. Liddle, *Nineteenth Century Delhi*, pp 282-85.
182. Liddle, *Nineteenth Century Delhi*, pp 285-86; Imdad Sabri, *1857 ke Mujahid Shoara*, Delhi 1959, p 203 onwards; R.M. Coopland, *A Lady's Escape from Gwalior and Life in the Fort of Agra During the Mutinies of 1857*, Smith, Elder & Co., London 1859, pp 268-69; Also see William Dalrymple, *The Last Mughal*, Penguin/Viking, New Delhi 2006, pp 424-26
183. Coopland, *A Lady's Escape*, pp 253-56, 263, 267; Norman and Young, *Delhi 1857*, p 297
184. Liddle, *Nineteenth Century Delhi*, p 290; Anjum ed. *Ghalib ke Khutut* vol 1 p 267; Ghalib, *Dastambu*, translated by Khwaja Ahmad Faruqi, Taraqqi Urdu Bureau, New Delhi 2000, p 66; *A Gazetteer of Delhi 1883-84*, p 207; Narayani Gupta, *Delhi Between Two Empires, 1803-1931*, Oxford University Press, New Delhi, 1981, pp 45-6
185. Liddle, *Nineteenth Century Delhi*, pp 290-91; Khaliq Anjum ed., *Ghalib ke Khutut*, Ghalib Institute, New Delhi 1985, vol 3 pp 993-4
186. Liddle, *Nineteenth Century Delhi*, p 291; *Testimonials, Sanads and Letters of Munshi Nathmal and of his Descendants*, p 6; Gupta, *Delhi Between Two Empires, 1803-1931*, pp 27-30, 39.

187. Arifi, *Shahar Ashob,, ek Tajzia*, p 222, translation mine
188. Delhi Commissioner's Office Records, 11/1860a
189. Gupta, *Delhi Between Two Empires, 1803-1931*, p 57
190. Gupta, *Delhi Between Two Empires, 1803-1931*, pp 84-85; Anthony D. King, *Colonial Urban Development: Culture, Social Power and Environment*, Routledge, London 2007, p 220
191. Gupta, *Delhi Between Two Empires, 1803-1931*, pp 29-30, 42-44
192. Bholanauth Chunder, *Travels of a Hindoo*, N Trubner & Co., London 1869, pp 389-90
193. Gupta, *Delhi Between Two Empires, 1803-1931*, pp 51-53, 81.
194. Gupta, *Delhi Between Two Empires, 1803-1931*, pp 70-3, 76, 80, 83
195. *A Gazetteer of Delhi 1883-84*, p 158, *A Gazetteer of Delhi 1912*, (Reprint) Aryan Books International, New Delhi, 2011, p 220; Sangat Singh, *Freedom Movement in Delhi (1858-1919)*, Associated Publishing House, New Delhi, 1972, pp 26-7.
196. Gupta, *Delhi Between Two Empires, 1803-1931*, pp 97-100; Singh, *Freedom Movement in Delhi*, pp 37-39.
197. Gupta, *Delhi Between Two Empires, 1803-1931*, pp 102-6, 136
198. J. Talboys Wheeler, *The History of the Imperial Assemblage at Delhi*, Longman, Green, Reader and Dyer, London, p xiii.
199. Gupta, *Delhi Between Two Empires, 1803-1931*, pp 108-9
200. The Viceroy, Lord Lytton, quoted in Bernard S. Cohn, 'Representing Authority in British India' in *An Anthropologist Among the Historians and Other Essays*, Oxford University Press, Delhi, 1994, p 656.
201. Cohn, 'Representing Authority', pp 661, 664
202. Cohn, 'Representing Authority', *passim*.
203. Cohn, 'Representing Authority', p 661
204. Val C. Prinsep, *Imperial India; An Artist's Journals*, Chapman and Hall, London 1878, pp 20, 29
205. Prinsep, *Imperial India*, p 22

206. Bashiruddin Ahmad, *Waqiat-e-dar-ul-hukumat-e-Dehli*, (Reprint) Urdu Academy, Delhi, 2001, vol 1, p 756; Cohn, 'Representing Authority', p 656; Kenneth W. Jones, 'Organized Hinduism in Delhi and New Delhi' in Frykenberg ed., *Delhi Through the Ages*, pp 206-7
207. Jones, 'Organized Hinduism', pp 207-12; Gupta, *Delhi Between Two Empires, 1803-1931*, pp 73-76, 129-34; Singh, *Freedom Movement in Delhi*, pp 42-7, 65
208. Singh, *Freedom Movement in Delhi*, pp 83-93
209. Gupta, *Delhi Between Two Empires, 1803-1931*, p 130
210. Gupta, *Delhi Between Two Empires, 1803-1931*, pp 136-40; Singh, *Freedom Movement in Delhi*, pp 92-93.
211. Singh, *Freedom Movement in Delhi*, pp 101-102
212. Singh, *Freedom Movement in Delhi*, pp 97-101
213. Gupta, *Delhi Between Two Empires, 1803-1931*, p 119, 143-45
214. Julie F. Codell, 'Photography and the Delhi Coronation Durbars: 1877, 1903, 1911' in Julie F. Codell ed. *Power and Resistance: The Delhi Coronation Durbars*, Mapin Publishing and the Alkazi Collection of Photography, Mumbai, 2012, pp 28-9, 37
215. James R. Ryan and Nicola J. Thomas, 'Landscapes of Performance: Staging the Delhi Durbars', in Codell ed. *Power and Resistance*, p 49.
216. Gupta, *Delhi Between Two Empires, 1803-1931*, pp 64, 160; *A Gazetteer of Delhi 1912*, p 195.
217. King, *Colonial Urban Development*, p 237.
218. Christopher Pinney, 'The Line and the Curve: Spatiality and Ambivalence in the 1903 Delhi Coronation Durbar', in Codell ed. *Power and Resistance*, p 204
219. Jim Masselos, 'The Great Durbar Crowds: The Participant Audience', in Codell ed. *Power and Resistance*, pp 192, 197.
220. Letter from Seton, Foreign Department Proceedings, (Political), National Archives of India, New Delhi, 5.12.1809, no 107

221. Bashiruddin Ahmad, *Waqiat-e-dar-ul-hukumat-e-Dehli*, p 814; Swapna Liddle, *Delhi: 14 Historic Walks*, Westland, New Delhi 2011, pp 255-56.
222. Bipan Chandra et. al., *India's Struggle for Independence*, Penguin, New Delhi 1989, pp 126-28
223. Gupta, *Delhi Between Two Empires, 1803-1931*, pp 148-51; Singh, *Freedom Movement in Delhi*, pp 131-33; *A Gazetteer of Delhi 1912*, p 196.
224. Ashok Jaitly, *St Stephen's College: A History*, Roli Books, New Delhi, 2006, pp 12-13; Daniel O'Conner, *A Clear Star: C.F. Andrews and India 1904-1914*, Chronicle Books, New Delhi 2005, pp 98-100
225. Singh, *Freedom Movement in Delhi*, pp 119, 123-24, 127-31
226. Singh, *Freedom Movement in Delhi*, p 135
227. Singh, *Freedom Movement in Delhi*, pp 136, 144-50; Chandra et. al., *India's Struggle for Independence*, p 142.
228. Codell, 'Photography and the Delhi Coronation Durbars', p 30; *The Historical Record of the Imperial Visit to India, 1911*, John Murray, London, 1914, p 60-61, 183-9
229. Stephen Legg, *Spaces of Colonialism: Delhi's Urban Governmentalities*, Blackwell, Malden 2007, pp 99-101; Singh, *Freedom Movement in Delhi*, pp 160-61
230. Codell, 'Photography and the Delhi Coronation Durbars', pp 24-5; Masselos, 'The Great Durar Crowds', pp 199-202
231. Singh, *Freedom Movement in Delhi*, pp 166-82, 238
232. Jaitly, *St Stephen's College,* pp 14, 16-21
233. Singh, *Freedom Movement in Delhi*, pp 221-onwards
234. Singh, *Freedom Movement in Delhi*, pp 242- ; Subhadra Sen Gupta, 'Lighting a Spark: The Story of Indraprastha School' in Narain Prasad and Subhadra Sen Gupta eds. *Indraprastha: The Quest for Women's Education in Delhi*, New Delhi 2012, pp 70-2
235. Chandra et al, *India's Struggle for Independence*, pp 181-82

236. Gupta, *Delhi Between Two Empires*, p 204
237. Gupta, *Delhi Between Two Empires*, pp 205-9; Singh, *Freedom Movement in Delhi*, pp 267-75
238. Gupta, *Delhi Between Two Empires, 1803-1931*, pp 214-20; Legg, *Spaces of Colonialism*, pp125-26; Jones, 'Organized Hinduism', pp 213-15
239. Gupta, *Delhi Between Two Empires, 1803-1931*, pp 57-60
240. Legg, *Spaces of Colonialism*, pp 151-65
241. Legg, *Spaces of Colonialism*, p 102
242. Gupta, *Delhi Between Two Empires, 1803-1931*, pp 55, 59-60, 64-5, 181-82; Legg, *Spaces of Colonialism*, pp 192.
243. Legg, *Spaces of Colonialism*, pp 178-9; *A Gazetteer of Delhi 1912*, p 220
244. Legg, *Spaces of Colonialism*, pp 193-96
245. Legg, *Spaces of Colonialism*, pp 196-204
246. Chandra et. al., *India's Struggle for Independence*, pp 248-50
247. Chandra et. al., *India's Struggle for Independence*, pp 248-50
248. Kavita A. Sharma and W.D. Mathur, *Hindu College Delhi: A People's Movement*, Niyogi Books, New Delhi, 2014, pp 29-31
249. Legg, *Spaces of Colonialism*, pp 111-12
250. David A. Johnson, *New Delhi: The Last Imperial City*, Palgrave MacMillan, Kindle edition, p 189
251. Legg, *Spaces of Colonialism*, pp 135-48
252. Kalyani Dutta, 'Stepping Out into the World: Indraprastha College and Higher Education for Women', in Prasad and Sen Gupta eds. *Indraprastha*, pp 129-31; Sharma and Mathur, *Hindu College Delhi*, pp 38-42
253. P.N. Chopra ed, *Quit India Movement: British Secret Report*, Thomson Press, Faridabad, 1976, pp 279-80
254. Legg, *Spaces of Colonialism*, pp 115-18
255. Chandra et. al., *India's Struggle for Independence*, pp 471-72, 475-79

256. Lionel Carter ed. *Partition Observed: British Official Reports from South Asia,* Manohar, New Delhi 2011, pp 67-8
257. Carter ed. *Partition Observed*, pp 100, 132, 152, 166-7
258. Carter ed. *Partition Observed*, p 173
259. Carter ed. *Partition Observed*, pp 183-85, 188, 193, 236.
260. Carter ed. *Partition Observed*, pp 285, 261, 349
261. Carter ed. *Partition Observed*, pp 324, 349, 390-91, 463, 533, 537, 720
262. Carter ed. *Partition Observed*, pp 314, 352
263. V.N. Datta, 'Panjabi Refugees and the Urban Development of Greater Delhi', in Frykenberg ed. *Delhi Through the Ages*, p 292.

www.ingramcontent.com/pod-product-compliance
Lightning Source LLC
Chambersburg PA
CBHW051117230426
43667CB00014B/2625